LAMBROS FATSIS
MELAYNA LAMB

POLICING
THE PANDEMIC

How Public Health Becomes Public Order

First published in Great Britain in 2022 by

Policy Press, an imprint of
Bristol University Press
University of Bristol
1-9 Old Park Hill
Bristol
BS2 8BB
UK
t: +44 (0)117 954 5940
e: bup-info@bristol.ac.uk

Details of international sales and distribution partners are available at
policy.bristoluniversitypress.co.uk

British Library Cataloguing in Publication Data
A catalogue record for this book is available from the British Library

ISBN 978-1-4473-6107-7 paperback
ISBN 978-1-4473-6108-4 ePub
ISBN 978-1-4473-6109-1 ePdf

Cover design: Bristol University Press
Front cover image: Saskia Vanderstichele

Bristol University Press and Policy Press use environmentally responsible
print partners.

Printed in Great Britain by CMP, Poole

Contents

About the authors

Lambros Fatsis is a Senior Lecturer in Criminology at the University of Brighton. His scholarly interests revolve around police racism and the criminalisation of Black music subcultures, fusing Cultural Criminology with Black radical thought. His co-authored book, *The Public and Their Platforms* (with Mark Carrigan), is published by Bristol University Press.

Melayna Lamb is a Lecturer at the University of Law, London. Her research interests span the fields and intersections of political philosophy, critical theory and Black radical thought. Her monograph, *A Philosophical History of Police Power* is forthcoming with Bloomsbury.

Acknowledgements

This book emerged *as a book* after Rebecca Tomlinson, Commissioning Editor at Bristol University Press, floated the idea to us, shortly after the first UK lockdown in March 2020.

What started as a series of discussions between the authors, and between us and the publisher, however, became a relationship that involved many more people, who took an interest in our work and encouraged us to start writing.

We would therefore wish to thank Rebecca for approaching us in the first place and everybody at Bristol University Press and Policy Press who waited patiently until we were ready to submit a manuscript that was a labour of love for us both.

We are also greatly indebted to Saskia Vanderstichele, who so generously agreed to let us use one of her photographs as the cover image for our book. Her work can be found at www.vanderstichele.net/

On a more personal note, we wish to thank our friend Rosa Marvell for introducing us to each other. Without her, we would probably never have met or had the chance to work together on this book.

Introduction

When a previously unknown pathogen (SARS-CoV-2) escalated into an unprecedented outbreak of the coronavirus disease (COVID-19) in January 2020, it was declared a 'public health emergency of international concern' by the Director General of the World Health Organization (WHO, 2020). Two months later, this deadly virus hit the UK as a reality that could no longer be ignored, downplayed or waved aside – even by a decidedly negligent government (Bradley et al, 2020; Monbiot, 2021). Amid a catalogue of dismal failures that exposed people to harm and led to record numbers of avoidable deaths (Lawrence, 2020; Stewart and Sample, 2020; Toynbee, 2021; Calvert and Arbuthnott, 2021), the UK government prioritised a law enforcement response which *treated the public as the virus*, instead of enforcing precautions to *protect the public from the virus* through a focus on healthcare and welfare.

These new regulations initially came in the form of a Coronavirus Bill, which passed through Parliament on 25 March 2020 and became law in the form of the Coronavirus Act 2020. This new legislation created an array of new police powers and was accompanied by a statutory instrument which gave legal force to the new social distancing rules. These rules prohibited people from 'leav[ing] the place where they are living without reasonable excuse'[1] during the lockdown and empowered the police to 'direct' or 'remove' individuals 'to the place where they are living'; allowing the use of 'reasonable force, if necessary'.[2] Breaching the prohibition amounted to 'commit[ting] an offence' which is 'punishable on summary conviction by a fine'.[3] Put simply, failure to comply with these instructions means breaking the law and, therefore, committing a crime – effectively turning fundamental rights and civil liberties such as freedom of movement and assembly into criminal offences.

Even after sixty-four revisions at the time of writing (Syal, 2021), these laws retained their status as law enforcement measures that 'proved a recipe for injustice'– threatening civil liberties and limiting the right to protest, using the pandemic as an excuse (Liberty, 2021: 6). Yet, the police relied on their new legal powers to impose fines, disperse gatherings, remove people to their homes, issue court summonses, resort to online shaming, deploy vehicle checkpoints, use aerial drones and roadblocks to enforce the lockdown and target Black people, other racialised minorities and anti-racist protesters during the #BlackLivesMatter demonstrations in the summer of 2020 (Fatsis, 2020; Netpol, 2020).

Using policing to manage public health emergencies at the expense of human rights and civil liberties, therefore, inevitably asserts itself as a major political problem that demands serious reflection. In the absence of any other alternative, arresting the spread of the virus through policing 'the public' would seem defensible to many – if policing were to merely supplement, rather than substitute, the adequate provision of healthcare. Introducing public health regulations to ensure compliance through law enforcement could therefore be justified, but only as a last resort – not as an alternative to a full-fledged public health strategy.

Lamentably, the onset of COVID-19 in the UK was largely treated as a *penal* rather than a *medical* matter, by decreeing legal restrictions rather than safeguarding public welfare. In so doing, a public health emergency was disguised as a public order issue through the introduction of new legislation instead of healthcare provision and welfare support. While these new laws (namely, The Health Protection (Coronavirus, Restrictions) (England) Regulations) are billed as health protection measures, emergency legislation which creates new offences and widens police powers does not – and cannot – limit the spread of infectious diseases. As public health experts dutifully remind us, what is required instead is a mix of 'scientific input, strong political commitment, and decisive action' (Baker et al, 2020: 2; Robert, 2020), not behavioural 'nudges' (Yates, 2020), evasiveness and dithering (Freedland, 2020). To make matters worse, relying on the enforcement of sanctions to protect people from vulnerability to harm is to allow criminal justice institutions to (re)define themselves as custodians of healthcare and welfare – in ways that blur the boundaries between law enforcement and medical care, to say nothing of the relationship between public health and public order.

The choice to *police* instead of to *protect* the public, however, does not just disguise a pandemic illness as a criminal act or allow the police to masquerade as care personnel, who just so happen to be armed with tasers, truncheons and other implements of violence. It also reveals a longstanding relationship between public health, welfare and policing that has scarcely been thought or talked about in the context of COVID-19 – notable exceptions notwithstanding (Benton, 2020; McQuade and Neocleous, 2020; Toscano, 2020). In response to such a curious silence on how and why 'public health' becomes 'public order', this book was written to show that public health and public order shade seamlessly into each other, because they share a common political history that doesn't go away just because we don't care to attend to it. Understanding why so much political energy was devoted to policing the COVID-19 pandemic, therefore, involves exploring the very ideological and historical origins of modern policing in Europe; as an institution that combines 'protection from danger' and a 'concern with matters of welfare' (Knemeyer and Trib, 1980: 182). Blending welfare and order maintenance functions, policing folds up 'order, security and welfare' into one category (Knemeyer and Trib, 1980: 182), making policing difficult to think away from how the state designs institutions and regulations of public welfare. In the context of the COVID-19 pandemic, this means that our thinking about how and why public health crises are policed as public order issues, requires a booster dose of history and critical analysis.

Written with this aim in mind, this book offers a critical discussion of policing that is set in its proper historical and political context; urging an urgent and timely rethinking of what policing *is*, what it *does*, who does it do it *to* and who does it to it *for*. As such, we take up issues that energised the most recent wave of #BlackLivesMatter protests – and its (over)policing (Netpol, 2020) – which also confounded sceptics, critics and mainstream punditry inside and outside academia. Addressed to those with a genuine interest in figuring out why policing is foregrounded in the mobilisations, slogans, protests and commentary against the policing of COVID-19, this book was written to be read as a companion, not a substitute, to such critiques from the streets. Our intention is not to replace 'struggle' with 'study', but to fuse the two together in the manner that Robin D.G. Kelley (2016) so inspiringly invites us to do.

If this book is written for those with an interest in breaking out of the established order that we are born and educated into, however, it is also written against those who defend such an unequal order in their capacity as citizens, criminal justice professionals or policing scholars. We refuse the notion that policing is not inherently and fundamentally political, and insist that scholarship which presents itself as 'neutral' should not be considered without a healthy dose of scepticism. While 'impartiality' may sound enticing to those who are convinced that they look at the social world around them by standing on neutral ground, we offer here a radical interrogation and critique of that ground. We therefore bring our (abolitionist) politics into our work, since the work we do is political.

Siding with C.L.R. James (2013: 18), we 'do not propose to be impartial'. Rather, we insist that '[a]ny public lecturer on politics who says he [*sic*] is impartial is either an idiot or a traitor'. 'You cannot be impartial in matters of this kind', as C.L.R. James categorically puts it. Pulling the political roots of policing out of it − or placing policing in a watertight container to vacuum up any trace of how it emerged, as what and who for − does not paint a neutral picture of a neutral object of analysis. It simply obscures what is already politically and ideologically charged, at the cost of factual error and misleading untruths; or what one of us calls 'dangerous myths and comfortable untruths' (Fatsis, 2019).

Those who are repulsed by, and become impatient with, tirades against policing, state violence and state power might wish to look away or stop reading. Yet, in the hope that you read on to find out more about why we hold such a critical view of policing, we address this book to those who are curious about the recent explosions in protest and transnational conversations about defunding and abolishing the police. Committed as we are to academic rigour, we would consider it dishonest to befog our readers with romantic fictions about the police as defenders of public safety and guarantors of a harmonious social order, when history tells a different story. If you are unfamiliar with these histories and critical analyses, we would therefore encourage you to read on and grapple with the historical function of policing: to serve and protect the maintenance of an unequal social order which requires their existence as the state's mercenaries or indeed as the state's prime 'coercion wielding' (Tilly, 1992: 1) institution. Having drawn a preliminary sketch of the book's main concerns and where we stand in relation to what we write about, the remainder of this introductory section outlines what each chapter does, offering a roadmap for the main contents of the book and introducing its main themes.

Chapter One opens the book with a discussion of what the policing of COVID-19 in the UK tells us about the nature, historical mission, function and purpose of British policing itself from the era of colonial slavery to the present day. Organised around two main arguments, this chapter focuses on how and why: (i) the police were called in because medical care was left out in the state's response to the ravages of COVID-19; and (ii) how public health is policed as a public order issue. Drawing on an analysis of why the public are policed as a virus and why we should rethink policing as a public threat, or a virus even, this chapter invites us to rethink why we are policed, how we are ruled and what the connections between the two are. The failure(s) of the UK government's chosen approach to COVID-19 will therefore be likened to a vivid illustration of policing political crises – taking a cue from the analysis by Hall et al (1982) of how the state manages political crises through law enforcement; showing force in order to assert its dominance and disguising state failure over adequate medical provision as a criminal justice matter where the public (instead of the virus) becomes the object of policy making.

Chapter Two moves against the current of mainstream opinion, commentary and criminological scholarship and sets out to explain how notions of public health are entwined with public order. By approaching public health and public order as mutually constitutive, this chapter argues that the question of who is to be protected is not a medical, but a political question. It can therefore only be understood by making sense of how the state and its criminal justice institutions define people in and 'out of the edifice of citizenship' (Dahrendorf, 1985: 98), thereby determining who deserves and who does not deserve protection both in terms of healthcare and overall welfare. This becomes obvious when the impact of both COVID-19 and the policing against the public is understood in terms of which 'public' is disproportionately affected by both. The most recent findings of disproportionality in COVID-19-related deaths among – and the police powers used against – Black and minority ethnic individuals serve as an illustration of the false dichotomy between public health and public order. By linking and thinking the two terms together, therefore, Chapter Two highlights that such disparities are neither random nor unavoidable. COVID-19 is therefore approached here as a health problem whose causes and responses are political rather than medical, recognising that even purely biological threats or natural catastrophes 'don't kill people randomly. They select victims in specific race, class and ethnic categories' (Becker, 2014: 153). Such public health emergencies occur against a backdrop of social and economic inequalities (Bambra et al, 2020) that are best understood if the political nature of public health and public order is understood, as this chapter argues based on an analysis of the historical and conceptual origins and institutional function of public health and public order institutions.

Chapter Three offers an alternative vision for designing public safety without and beyond policing. Drawing on abolitionist scholarship, this chapter makes the case for disarming, disbanding and defunding the police (McDowell and Fernandez, 2018) for just, sustainable and inclusive solutions to public safety. Instead of responding to social and political problems through law enforcement, health emergencies included, we argue against policy making that prioritises suspicion, surveillance, punitiveness, stigmatisation or coercion over investment in healthcare, welfare, social solidarity and mutual aid. In so doing, a series of misconceptions and falsehoods about the role and mission of the criminal justice system in protecting the public are dismissed as factually and empirically false, as well as ethically and politically dubious. We therefore draw on overwhelming evidence that demonstrates that not only do criminal justice institutions consistently fail at their stated objectives, but that they are also the wrong institutions to rely on for protecting the public's welfare, healthcare and safety. Based on a rich Black radical tradition and its abolitionist agenda from 19th century to the present day, this final chapter offers a critique of law and order scholarship and politics, while also proposing a positive and reconstructive alternative that demonstrates how we can still have public safety without and beyond policing.

If we were to offer a snapshot of this book's content in just one paragraph, we would probably say that it draws its sense of purpose from a desire to critique policing and to insist that designing public safety, be it from violence or infectious diseases, is not – and should not be – the property of the police. It can (also) be practised in non-coercive means through investment in healthcare, or upheld through social solidarity and mutual aid, not tainted by suspicion, surveillance, punitiveness or shaming. This involves thinking about policing away from the received unwisdom we have been educated into from an early age; thereby heeding Raymond Chandler's (1977: 599) oft-quoted – but otherwise largely ignored – observation that 'cops are like a doctor that gives you aspirin for a brain tumor, except that the cop would rather cure it with a blackjack'. The 'blackjack' solution to social problems or pandemic diseases should therefore be rejected, not only because it is short-sighted, ill-thought, insufficient or misplaced, but because it is violent and causes inordinate harm. If crime is a symptom, then the condition that causes it lies deeper than the police could ever do anything about, other than beat us into the 'legal and political order of the state' (Hall et al, 1982: 201–8).

ONE

Policing 'the public' as a virus

The preceding pages of this book introduced it as a critique of policing and state power in times of political and public health crisis – that the onset of COVID-19 made clear for all to see. To be true to its promise, this chapter will expand on why both policing itself and the policing of the public as a virus is a political problem that needs to be rethought away from diehard clichés that obscure what policing is, what it does, who does it do it to and who does it do it for. As such, this chapter is not – nor does it proffer the pretence of being – a treatise on public health, epidemiology or immunology. Rather, this chapter offers a critique of policing in the context of a pandemic.

Anchored in the – admittedly and deliberately provocative – assertion that the public is policed as a contaminated entity that needs to be controlled, instead of being approached as a population that needs protection from the risk of infection, this chapter pursues two interrelated arguments. The first argument that is put forward, which informs the general tenor of this book, is that – in the UK – the police were called in because medical care was left out in the state's response to the ravages of COVID-19. As a result of such political decision making, the policing of the public over protecting the public from a deadly virus transformed a public health emergency into a public order priority. In the light of such (mis)handling of a public health crisis, it becomes clear that the challenges that any pandemic brings in its wake are medical as well as political, given that it is political decisions that shape how resources are allocated and what institutions are empowered to respond to sudden emergency situations.

The second argument that informs this chapter, speaks to the political nature of how public health is policed as a public order issue. It invites readers to rethink why we are policed, how we are ruled, what the connections between the two are, and how to escape the confines of such a political predicament. Both arguments are situated in their proper historical context, to demonstrate that the politics behind the policing of COVID-19 – much like policing itself – has its roots in Britain's colonial past; in the absence of which, policing would be, look and feel different to how it does.

The two arguments that shape the remainder of this chapter are introduced by two corresponding slogans that criticise the law and order politics adopted by various national states across the globe in response to COVID-19. Although these two slogans have been encountered by the authors online and in particular European countries – namely, Greece and Belgium – they have also featured in the form of graffiti, stickers and posters around the world, including Britain. Before introducing them, a health warning might be required – especially for those who abhor facile clichés as much as we do. These two slogans may look, think and feel like mere boilerplates of left-revolutionary agitators. The reality they reflect, however, is equally commonplace – although it does not elicit the same disapproval, making the way the world is currently put together look as if it is immune to, or beyond, critique. We therefore draw on these two slogans for their ability to dramatise and spotlight social and political realities that are normalised, legitimised and absorbed into our language and modes of thinking – so much so that they become invisible and unquestioned; like pieces of familiar mental furniture that upholster our socio-cultural and political life. While we make no excuses for committing them to paper and weaving our thinking around them – by owning up to their oversimplification of the matters at hand – we also disown the socio-political and cultural order that these short and striking phrases castigate. We therefore merely mention them here, as a way of capturing our readers' attention, before we provide some elaboration in turn. To do them justice, we encourage readers to think of them in their proper context – on walls and in public – and see them as illustrations of the two arguments that shape this chapter and give it its critical edge too:

- Slogan 1: *'Police units everywhere, intensive care units nowhere'*
- Slogan 2: *'The police are the virus'*.

'Police units everywhere, intensive care units nowhere': policing the public as a virus

After a summer of lockdown easing followed by a rise in infections and a heavier police presence in city streets, protesters in Greece marched against the prioritisation of policing over medical care – holding aloft banners and flyers that carried the slogan: 'Police Units Everywhere, Intensive Care Units Nowhere' (*MAT παντού, MEΘ πουθενά*). Both the slogan – which juxtaposes similar-sounding words for police or Order Restoration Units (*MAT*/ORU) and Intensive Care Units (*MEΘ*/ICU) – and the critique it expresses, are testimony to political decisions that call on 'cops' to stand in for 'docs' in the midst of a global pandemic. Not unlike the UK, law enforcement in Greece and elsewhere took the place of frontline healthcare; revealing how and why states see their public as *suspects* who need to be policed, rather than as *patients* who need to be protected from an infectious disease.

This may sound like a sweeping assertion. However, it is also a fact that offers valuable insights into how and why material resources (= money) and power (= authority) are allocated the way they are and why certain institutions (for example the police) are relied on more than others (for example healthcare). Such (unequal) distribution of resources, ordering of (democratic?) political power, and structuring of (public!) institutional arrangements is not accidental, but written into our political institutions and culture. Indeed, such socio-economic and political configurations help us to understand how political systems create the world we live in, but they also remind us that the organisation of resources, power and institutional infrastructures is not preordained, immaculately conceived or metaphysically imposed. On the contrary, the (mis)management of money, power and people is created as a result of specific human processes of decision making that bear the imprint of political ideology; that is to say, ways of looking at and reacting to the world from a particular perspective and social location. To put it somewhat bluntly, we get (coercive) policing instead of (supportive) care because of political ideologies of law and order that are shared across the established political spectrum (Gilroy and Sim, 1987; Fatsis, 2021a), albeit in differing degrees.

Such a realisation amounts to more than recognising that the public is policed as a virus because the state fails to protect and support the public from a virus, although this is a crucial point that bears repeating. Confronting this discomfiting truth also alerts us to telltale signs of political crisis, where state power expands to defend itself from its own failures and from the possibility of challenge by the very public that the state has failed to protect. Doubling down on law enforcement at the expense of public health provision makes sense when – in times of crisis – the state realises that the only option is to rush to police those whom it cannot protect. Policing, therefore, takes over when a public health infrastructure is allowed to crumble. Since the state cannot rely on an infrastructure it has wilfully abandoned, neglected and withdrawn proper investment in and support for, suppressing the public overrides the suppression or – better still – the elimination of a virus. Simply put, the conundrum that haunts the state in the face of an emergency is resolved swiftly and decisively, by exercising its political will to fortify state power through law enforcement, rather than build up public welfare through medical and social support.

This is not an exception to how states think and act. This *is* the way states think and act, however invisible this political logic may be in times of 'normality', real or imaginary. Lack of sufficient investment in frontline healthcare, welfare provision, emergency preparedness and shortages in medical equipment that spell out the absence of a range of adequate health, social and economic support measures, are nothing new. However, we only really feel the pinch when the chips are down in times of impending *crisis*, restlessness and reaction, not in periods of relative *stasis*, passivity and inaction. Or, to be more precise, some only feel the pinch in times of crisis (= white, affluent people), while others feel the pinch all the time, crisis or no crisis.

When this (always belated) realisation dawns on us, failures in state support are (re)presented as a casualty of emergencies and crises, not as the product of state failure. What is a default setting, therefore, is mistaken for a system error to draw attention away from a (f)ailing public health and social infrastructure. Things become even more complicated, and perhaps more worrying, when the state pretends that public health is prioritised even if it is (mis)handled by and handed to the wrong personnel, thereby wrapping the iron fist of law and order with the velvet glove of public health. The UK government's (self-)justification of the Coronavirus Bill as a public health response in March 2020 is a good case in point. Although the government proposed its Coronavirus Bill before it became an Act (in law), it was proposed as a change in legislation 'for the purposes of preventing, protecting against, controlling or providing a public health response to the incidence or spread of infection or contamination'. So far so good, yet the cast list of 'relevant persons' for enforcing these regulations is limited to 'constables, police community support officers (PCSOs)' or 'those designated by local authorities and by the Secretary of State'. Given that COVID-19 is a public health threat, it might be sensible to suggest that it requires medical attention from healthcare personnel rather than intervention by criminal justice institutions. So why are doctors and nurses not deemed equally or more 'relevant' professionals, compared to police officers? Or to paraphrase, ever so slightly, why is the government trying to 'police its way out of a pandemic', as the civil liberties organisation, Liberty, aptly puts it – in a trenchant critique of the government's Coronavirus Act (Liberty, 2021: 10)? The shortest possible answer that we can muster is that policing medical emergencies, instead of caring for or looking after those who are affected by them, is easier, cheaper and comes naturally to the state, whose priority is to make 'the public' more governable, not safer.

Order trumps safety when the state feels threatened, because what is seen as a threat is not the effect of a virus on the health or welfare of its citizens, but the effect that a virus has on shaking the state's power, authority and legitimacy. When crises suddenly hit, patterns of bad governance and misrule – that otherwise go unnoticed in the daily routine of social life – gradually become visible. It is *this* threat that the state rushes to respond to, by bolting itself to the power that ensures its survival, instead of unlocking (re)sources of support for its citizens.

This may sound overly provocative or unjustifiably suspicious and mistrustful towards the nature, logic, politics and workings of state rule; thereby signalling a wholesale dismissal of, attack on or threat to, 'our' political institutions. This observation, however, is offered as a timely – yet long overdue – opportunity to abandon delusions that lure us into thinking that we have the political arrangements we need and want; pricking us instead with a healthy dose of radical doubt, rooted in thinking about how existing political institutions become *instituted* in the first place, by whom and for what.

Instead of looking at the onset of COVID-19 as a medical crisis with political implications, we would like to encourage an approach that allows us to see, make sense of and recognise this moment as profoundly political – despite the fact that it took a medical emergency of global proportions to expose the fault lines of our political systems of governance. Doing so, opens up the possibility of understanding why the state perceives such emergencies as crises that mount a challenge to its legitimacy, instead of responding to such crises as something that the state ought to challenge to protect its citizens. Seen this way, the choice of policing the pandemic away reveals a political crisis that is handled by way of (law and) order, not by way of protection, care and support.

Echoing Mike Davis' (2020: 11) illustrative description of our current predicament as a 'medical Katrina', it seems useful to rethink COVID-19 as a worrying example of how medical disasters are blamed for a failing and long-neglected public health and social infrastructure. Not unlike Hurricane Katrina, in whose wake New Orleans was submerged as floodwater overflowed – due to infrastructure neglect that caused the federal levees to break – the onset of COVID-19 also proved to be catastrophic; not on its own, but aided by state disinvestment in the social service safety net. In other words, the political decision making that precedes disasters like Hurricane Katrina or COVID-19 prepares the ground for, facilitates and enables such disasters to cause the great damage and losses that they do. What lies beneath the drowning of New Orleans in 2005 by Hurricane Katrina and the casualties of COVID-19, therefore, is not just the *un*natural and non-medical source of devastation; this being no other than state absenteeism and political irresponsibility.[1] Both cases also highlight how and why the state prioritised the policing of its citizens, rather than protecting them. Just as Louisiana's Governor, Kathleen Blanco, sent National Guard troops to police rather than rescue the Crescent City's predominantly African American citizens, the legal machinery of the British state was also set in motion to prioritise the creation of new punishable offences, instead of boosting healthcare provision and welfare support. Shocking though such realisation may be, it should hardly occasion surprise, given that state failure is nothing new – no matter how invisible its responsibility might seem until disasters hit.

Equally, the political nature of medical crises should also not be seen as a revelation, given that medical issues are inescapably political – as the historical scholarship of Christopher Hamlin (2006) and Michel Foucault (1973) helpfully reminds us. To separate the medical from the political realm would be to divorce health from the state institutions that administer it through (political) decision-making processes and their casualties. So related are the two, that philosopher Michel Foucault (1973: 33) felt confident enough to argue that 'the struggle against disease must begin with a war against bad government'. Casting doubt about the intention of the state to allocate resources for the benefit of its citizens might sound unfair to the state institutions we have been socialised into thinking as normal and unproblematic, forgetting perhaps that we have been *institutionalised* into such institutions through(out) our education (nurseries, schools, universities) and other aspects of our social life. These include the way we earn a living (the workplace), find shelter (housing), access healthcare (hospitals, clinics, surgeries), make our political voice heard (parliament), and indeed get punished for breaking the law (police stations, detention centres, courtrooms, prisons). The familiarity that all such institutional arrangements inspire, renders them invisible as potentially problematic ways of organising social life.

Indeed, their familiarity tricks us into thinking that the institutions of social life we currently have are the *only* ones we could have and need, or that the *only* way to create and experience social life is through (such) institutions. The danger that such thinking poses is that thinking with and through such institutions discourages us from thinking how and why existing institutions of social life were *instituted*. By whom? To do what? To whom? For whom? Answering these questions requires us to rethink the state as a unit of political organisation that is not the neutral container we mistake it for, but a politically charged outcome of processes that 'make' power, authority, dominance and rule.

At the heart of such a critical stance towards the state lies the realisation that state power is revealed to unpoliced populations only in times of crisis. For such populations, it is only periods of crisis that lay bare what is otherwise normal(ised) in the lives of those who are excluded, marginalised, criminalised, policed and confined. As the state's coercive power remains invisible to those who can afford to 'unsee' and ignore it, public health crises nevertheless teach us that 'it is the behaviour of governments, more than the behaviour of the virus or individuals, that shapes countries' experience of the crisis' (Baker and McKee, 2021).

When the British government was challenged by the COVID-19 crisis, it chose to move in the direction of law and order in order to contain an imploding political crisis, by disguising a pathogen as a problem to be solved by law enforcement – as if it were a crime. It would not be an exaggeration to claim that this is a textbook case of a crisis of legitimacy as a result of state failure, and it would not be inaccurate to stress that law and order politics becomes a suitable way of managing such a crisis of state legitimacy. *This* is how and why public health crises become public order issues.

In such a context, COVID-19 offers a contemporary example with which to think about Foucault's (1995: 197) description of how 'the plague is met by order' through a range of 'disciplinary mechanisms' that include 'surveillance and control' and 'an intensification [...] of power' (Foucault, 1995: 211, 198). Not unlike the 17th-century plague that Foucault was writing about, COVID-19 also provides the setting or 'the trial in the course of which one may define ideally the exercise of disciplinary power' (Foucault, 1995: 198). The type of power that Foucault is referring to here is the power to 'make rights and laws' in a situation where the public instead of the virus becomes the object of policy making: '[i]nspection functions ceaselessly. The gaze is alert everywhere: "A considerable body of militia, commanded by good officers and men of substance", guards at the gates, at the town hall and in every quarter to ensure the prompt obedience of the people and the most absolute authority of the magistrates' (Foucault, 1995: 195–6).

Facile though it would be to suggest an(y) equivalence between the plague that Foucault was commenting on and COVID-19, the making of laws created offences during COVID-19 is not dissimilar to the way that 'the plague gave rise to disciplinary projects' (Foucault, 1995: 198). The 'strict spatial partitioning' in Foucault resembles our social distancing rules and the 'orde[r] to stay indoors' brings our experience of lockdowns to mind, in ways that allow comparisons between the logic of the orders that captured Foucault's attention and the 'type of government by executive decree' (Ewing, 2020: 1) that we witnessed on our shores.

It is worth remembering at this point that The Health Protection (Coronavirus, Restrictions) (England) Regulations came into force in 2020 'without parliamentary approval' (Ewing, 2020: 2) and with 'far-reaching consequences' for 'personal liberty', 'police powers' and 'political freedom' (Ewing, 2020: 1, 2), raising serious concerns about how a 'public health emergency' became the 'occasion for a suspension of constitutional government' (Ewing, 2020: 2). Bringing Foucault's pioneering of plagues and surveillance to bear on our Coronavirus-infected times allows us to conceptualise, contextualise and perhaps rebel against the ways in which authoritarian regimes of governance take shape. Nothing could summarise our predicament better than another except from Foucault's reminder that '[t]he plague as a form, at once real and imaginary, of disorder had as its medical and political correlative, discipline' (Foucault, 1995: 197–8).

To better understand how we are governed through policing, surveillance and other penal, carceral and disciplinary mechanisms, it might be useful to admit that the forms of emergency governance that we experience during crises are not unlike the forms of governance that apply to normal times. The main difference is that in times of emergency we pay closer attention, because some feel the presence of the state more. Yet it is the same state doing the same things that it did before our crisis-ridden times, albeit with less intensity or perhaps less noticeably for some. As Ewing (2020: 2) notes, there is a 'relationship between the COVID-19 crisis and the populism and authoritarianism that some had witnessed in the period immediately before the crisis'. Much of what Foucault describes as governance during plagues, therefore, applies to periods of normality, if we care to inquire into what government means, is and does.

Understanding the limits of our power over the institutions of state power that effectively rule how social life is lived, should therefore set off a deep and long overdue reckoning with the forms of politics we currently have, thereby inviting the question of whether this is the form of politics we need and want. Asking that question holds the key to understanding how a public health crisis like the COVID-19 pandemic shows our unthinking reliance on state power – and why exercising restraint over the public (instead of reducing the severity of a threat to public welfare) is not a deviation from, but an expression of, the institutional arrangements of political power that we live our lives by.

Rethinking public health emergencies as fundamentally political problems, therefore, poses a challenge to the way mainstream politics is conducted and understood, and to just how much of it goes unchallenged. This includes the making and enforcement of law at the expense of public welfare. With this thought in mind, we now turn to the historical mission, function and purpose of policing itself as a virus that is mistaken as a cure in the popular imagination – and in mainstream policing scholarship too.

'The police are the virus': policing as a public threat

In 2020, amid a nationwide lockdown on Easter weekend, 19-year old Adil was killed in the Anderlecht municipality of Brussels, when his scooter collided with a police car, whose drivers called for reinforcements. The reason? Adil fled a coronavirus check, for fear of a €250 fine. Soon afterwards, graffiti was sprayed on the region's walls – addressed to Adil and carrying the words: Adil, *le virus c'est la police* [Adil, the virus is the police]. The slogan[2] and the incident that it responds to, pose as many questions about policing as they answer. So let us take up a few in turn.

Should fear of a fine lead to death? Indeed, should the price of a fine determine whether someone lives or dies? Were reinforcements needed? Why? Who/what was the threat? What is the justification for relying on the police to enforce confinement and social distancing measures? Aren't such fatalities expected when *police forces* are sent out to en*force* the law? Was Adil helped by measures of supported isolation, instead of punitive law enforcement? How did the actions of the police keep 'the public' safe on this occasion? Why was the graffiti dedicated to Adil removed so quickly, but the police powers that led to his death remained in place? Which 'public' was kept safe? From whom and from what?

Let us try to address these questions, by quoting two policing scholars of radically different political persuasions, whose views nevertheless converge on what policing is, what it does, who it does it to and who does it do it for. Abolitionist sociologist of policing, Alex Vitale, whose book *The End of Policing* soared on bestseller lists in summer 2020 – in the wake of the most recent wave of #BlackLivesMatter protests – argues: 'The reality is that the police exist primarily as a system for managing and even producing inequality by ... tightly managing the behaviors of poor and nonwhite people: those on the losing end of economic and political arrangements' (Vitale, 2017: 36).

The second scholar is the renowned stalwart of policing studies David Bayley, whose political persuasions are decidedly more reformist. Yet, he categorically states:

> The police do not prevent crime. This is one of the best kept secrets of modern life. Experts know it, the police know it, but the public does not know it. Yet the police pretend that they are society's best defense against crime and continually argue that if they are given more resources, especially personnel, they will be able to protect communities against crime. This is a myth. ... Governments should either resolve the doubts about the usefulness of the police or face up to the conclusion that preventing crime requires a great deal more than pouring money into law enforcement. (Bayley, 1996: 3, 10)

Even a cursory glance at these quotes complicates conventional images of the police as benevolent 'crime-fighters'. What emerges instead is an understanding of the police as the state's front-line order maintenance institution. Reading the two quotes again, more carefully this time, questions about what laws are enforced, how they are enforced and how just they actually are, start percolating – and the established mythologies about policing that previously achieved the status of gospel truth, are now placed under proper critical scrutiny. Such a shift in perception, awareness and consciousness of the role of the police might feel disorienting. Yet, it is also necessary, if we want to stop relying on fallacies and misleading stock images of policing and 'crime' that are damaging to our understanding of both policing and crime. Placing policing and 'crime' in their proper historical and political context (instead of idealised conceptions or downright falsehoods), is a necessary step. What follows, therefore, is such a retelling of British police history. It resists and confronts dangerous myths and comfortable untruths – focusing instead on outlining the historical mission, function and role of the police as an order maintenance institution that bears the scars of Britain's imperial past, and bares its teeth at the postcolonial nation's 'suspect populations'.

To do so, the remainder of this chapter disrupts romanticised idea(l)s of policing as a neutral, benevolent, apolitical crime-fighting state institution. Such a rosy and happy imagery is replaced with a bleaker portrayal of the police as enforcers of order and a public threat, due to the coercive, violent nature of the job that the state employs the police for. This argument on policing is organised around a provocation that is intended to arouse curiosity about a fundamental, yet nevertheless uneasy, truth about policing – namely, that it is not a crime-fighting institution, but an order *creating* and order maintenance institution. To explore this undermined aspect of policing, we situate this provocation historically as a way of highlighting that the history of how institutions are made determines what they do at present, unless their historic mission, function and purpose is undone. Regrettably, policing is held hostage by its own institutional, social and political history. It therefore emerges in this chapter as a problematic institution to be eliminated, rather than as a benevolent and kindly institution that eliminates, solves or responds to social problems. As such, the remainder of the final section of this chapter upsets unquestioned common sense, or undue reverence for the kind of state-sponsored 'violence work' (Seigel, 2018) that we otherwise know as policing. Yet, we hope that it will inspire a fresh outlook with which to approach policing as a public threat; a state institution that enforces a rule of law that is as unjust as the power structure it upholds and legislates for.

Having already encountered David Bayley's (1996: 3) explosive assertion that 'the police do not prevent crime', we are now forced to grapple with its implications, to better understand what policing is. According to Ian Loader (2020: 10), 'the claim that the police mission is crime-fighting to be at best partial, more likely wishful fantasy. To call the police crime-fighters is to radically misunderstand the nature of policing'.[3] Part of the reason why such wishful thinking shapes our (mis)understanding of policing has to do with the fact that policing is an 'institution onto and through which people project various hopes and aspirations, fears and fantasies, about the social world' (Loader, 2020: 11). Such fantasies, however, are not random views from nowhere. They have a specific social and political history that open new vistas for our understanding of how we came to have the criminal justice institutions that we currently have, why they were 'made' or *instituted* this way, by whom and for what. To rebuff 'familiar truth-denying truisms' (Williams, 1993: 28) about policing, however, we need historical perspective – but not the kind that distorts our view when we see the world through 'imperialized eyes' (Bambara, 1992: xii). By contrast, we shall navigate an imperial-colonial history of British policing that is rarely taught or learnt because of the prickly issues it ushers in. Offered here are the outlines of an approach that can uncover and rescue this history from 'the enormous condescension of posterity' (Thompson, 1966: 12).

From colonial overseers to Metropolitan officers: British policing in historical perspective

The usual history of British policing follows a familiar refrain that goes like this: the police in Britain emerge as an institutionalised force with the formation of the London Metropolitan Police in 1829 by Sir Robert Peel, after whom the proverbial 'Bobbies' are named. The story quickly gains momentum, by adding a familiar plot line, which informs us that this "new" police force was founded in response to public unrest (Neocleous, 2000), rising crime (Taylor, 1997; Reiner, 2010) and as an instrument of discipline (Cohen, 1979; Storch,

1993) to keep the industrial(ised) working class in check. More sophisticated accounts go further, by offering some context into how the advent of industrial capitalism required the suppression of non-productive or leisurely pursuits (Storch, 1977). Such accounts point to how the English working class was beaten into submission and into conforming to the demands of industry – not just as a productive force which keeps economic activity alive, but as a moral imperative too. Industriousness, however, was not just productive and profitable for the industrial capitalists. It was also a sign of propriety, restraint and other straight-laced Victorian values of prudishness and high-toned moral superiority. This being the socio-cultural and historical context in which policing became professionalised, the social 'unrest' that policing was born to suppress was a response to 'deskilling' as a result of industrialisation, the 'crime' was the recreational use of public space and the 'discipline' administered mostly took the form of preventative beat patrolling, to root out 'inappropriate' (for which, read: non-industrious) behaviour in public.

More severe measures, however, were not uncommon, which the Peterloo Massacre of 1819 demonstrates. In fact, it became '[t]he signal event that showed the need for a professional police force' (Vitale, 2017: 38) to clamp down on the political activity of rebels like the Luddites – who destroyed their tools to protest against the replacement of skilled work by industrial machinery – or the Chartists, who advocated work reform for the impoverished and exploited English workers. What the '[o]riginal police force' – as Vitale (2017: 38) calls it – was created for, therefore, was to police the unproductive occupation of public space by working-class people (the proletariat). This involved making them work for a living in factories, coercing them into accepting their lower station in the emerging capitalist social hierarchy, and removing any obstacles to the efficient operation of mass-produced manufactured goods and the profits that are made by trading or selling such goods commercially.

While this rendering of British policing is not entirely false, it amounts to a near-total erasure of the imperial-colonial context within which all such economic, socio-cultural and political activity emerged. What is neglected is that the policing of the English white working class was modelled after the policing of colonial (surplus) populations in the British colonies of Ireland, the Caribbean and the Indian subcontinent (Arnold, 1986; Brogden, 1987; Das and Verma, 1998; Brown, 2002; Williams, 2003; Bell, 2013; Emsley, 2014; Jackson, 2016). Even when the role of the police as 'domestic missionaries' (Storch, 1993) is acknowledged, their pre-professional colonial predecessors are seldom mentioned in mainstream narratives.

This produces a confusing and confused historiography, which sees Britain as an industrial(ised) capitalist nation that is somehow disconnected from the ways in which industrial growth in English cities was 'financed by profits from the triangular [slave] trade' (Fryer, 1993: 15). It is therefore worth remembering that the iron industries, railways as well as the systems of banking and insurance that made capitalism possible, largely relied on the colonial economics of the slave trade (Fryer, 1993: 16; see also Williams, 1996; Baucom, 2005). As Erin D. Somerville (in Dabydeen et al, 2007: 37) notes: '[t]he triangular shipping route of the slave trade largely formed the banking industry in England', while the 'insurance market is believed to have begun at Edward Lloyd's coffee house in London' as a space where 'sailors, shipowners, and merchants … met to discuss private insurance arrangements' and a place where 'runaway slaves could be returned'. Even familiar high-street banks like Barclays Bank and the Bank of England had their 'capital tied to sugar and slave merchants' (Somerville in Dabydeen et al, 2007: 37). The connection between the slave trade and Britain's banking and insurance system could not be better or more callously demonstrated than the fate of the *Zong*, the British slave ship that carried '132 African slaves that were thrown overboard for insurance money' that ship-owners could claim on 'slaves dying of unnatural causes, including drowning to prevent rebellion or to ensure the safety of the ship and crew' (Dabydeen et al, 2007: 534, see also Walvin, 2011).

This was not the only connection between imperial Britain and its colonies. Rather, this is the very context in which capitalism developed and whose interests policing served. The neat separation of the history of policing in Britain from the history of such policing in Britain's colonies can only be thought of, rather charitably, as a case of cognitive dissonance or, less forgivably, as an unpardonable blind spot in police scholarship. Given that capitalism was a political-economic system built on colonial exploitation, it could not *only* affect the English working class without also affecting those who laboured in the colonies of British capitalism. Besides, as Fryer (1993: 17) notes, 'the emerging industrial working class in Britain was exploited [and policed] by the same capitalist class that exploited [and policed] black slaves'.

To trace the birth of British policing to 1820s London without making a connection to the fact that what happens in mainland Britain is inevitably informed by what is happening in its colonies, is to think of imperial Britain as a non-imperial nation. When the Met was founded in London, the slave trade may have ended, but the capitalist system of slavery itself was still alive and well – a decade after the official origin story of British policing.[4] This is important as a reminder of the fact that it is impossible to discuss or think about developments in Britain's internal affairs – like the formation of a professional police force, for example – without realising that this happens *in an imperial context*, which by definition requires the existence of colonies. It should therefore come as no surprise to hear that the metropolitan police force that we know as the Met is in fact the reincarnation of pre-professional colonial, slave-catching militias, with the plantation *overseer* being the forerunner of the metropolitan *officer*. As mainstream police historians remain dishonourably silent on this fact, it is interesting to note that rappers – who, like the enslaved, become 'police property' (Fatsis, 2021b) – were quick to draw such parallels. A case in point, is KRS-One's (1993) anthemic *Sound of Da Police*, which makes that connection between the 'officer who patrols the nation' and the 'overseer who rode in the plantation'. This detour, with old school hip hop as our guide and our soundtrack too, may seem fanciful. Yet, it treads where police historiography barely treads water; exposing an unwillingness to connect policing in the heart of the Empire as 'an all-purpose lever of urban discipline' (Storch, 1993: 282) to how policing England's working-class poor has its prehistory in the 'slave-hunting gangs hired by the West India sugar planters' (Fryer, 1993: 9).

To separate the one from the other is to divorce the history of British policing from its historical context. The history of British policing *is* imperial-colonial in nature – as it emerged in that very context. Contrary to conventional wisdom and mainstream criminological historiography, therefore, policing was not immaculately conceived in 19th-century London, but founded during colonialism and slavery. The models and styles of policing that emerged in the metropole derive from pre-professional, informal militias that were formed to patrol, capture and control fugitive slaves and colonial subjects in Britain's overseas 'possessions'. In fact, as Elsa Goveia (1960: 82) succinctly argued, 'the experience of the British colonies makes it particularly clear that police regulations lay at the very heart of the slave system and that, without them, the system became impossible to maintain'.

The antecedents of the London Metropolitan Police in 1829, therefore, exist not just in the Royal Irish Constabulary – also founded by Robert Peel in the former British colony of Ireland – but in the plantations of the Caribbean and the Indian subcontinent too. As such, police forces start their life as instruments of suppression – wielded by slaveholders and colonisers to maintain a form of discrimination, dehumanisation and violent subjugation (racial slavery) –

before evolving into professional institutions that serve and protect the state from those who are seen as undeserving of its protection. Originally designed to brutalise and terrorise slaves and colonial subjects, pre-professional colonial policing transitioned into professional institutionalised policing, targeting the same 'suspect populations' though comparable methods of 'penal excess' (Brown, 2002).

The role of the police: fight crime or enforce order?

Now that we know that, historically, the police do not fight crime but enforce order, it seems reasonable to ask what kind of 'order' that is. The *order* that policing as an order maintenance institution *maintains* is the order of an imperial-colonial state; both at home (see, for example, Storch, 1975) and in the Empire's colonial outposts (see, for example: Craton, 1982; Robinson, 1984; Linebaugh, 2006, 221; Robinson, 2020, 121–64). After all, resistance to policing at the seat of the Empire was also connected to the political activity that brewed in its colonies. For example, the origins of the working-class movement in England is seen as *white* (and) *English*, yet Black radicals played a key part in it. This serves as a reminder of the dangers and the error of disconnecting the 'imperial centre' from its 'colonial periphery', when the connective tissue between them is not geography proper but *political* geography – that is to say, politics.

As Fryer (1993: 48) highlights, 'black people play[ed] a part in the emerging British radical working-class movement' as much as 'British workers, especially after the Haitian revolution, ma[de] abolition one of their central aims'. Indeed, as Linebaugh (2006: 415) notes, the formerly enslaved Olaudau Equiano – author of *The Interesting Narrative of the Life of Olaudah Equiano or Gustavus Vassa, the African* – did much to 'prod[d]' and 'assis[t]' the abolitionist movement in England. So much so, that Linebaugh (2006: 415) argues that E.P. Thompson's history of *The Making of the English Working*

Class should be more accurately renamed: 'the making of the working class in England'; thereby calling attention to the absence of Equiano from the pantheon of working-class radicalism in England. What these examples illustrate is that the hierarchies of order that the police serve(d), are the *same* order across the Empire – although the 'public and psychological wage' of whiteness (Du Bois, 1936: 700) acted as a protective shield from the brutal dehumanising violence that was directed at the enslaved. Such wages of whiteness cash in on a combination of force, coercion and repression (through policing) with the accumulation of wealth (through trade); thereby calling for a reinterpretation of policing as involving 'law and economics, the protection of property and the protection of production' (Linebaugh, 2006: 427).

This is best illustrated by reference to another precursor of the Met: the River Thames Police – situated not in Africa, the Caribbean or the Indian subcontinent, but in the beating heart of the Empire. Not unlike the Met, the River Thames Police emerged within, and was shaped by, the same imperial-colonial context – not least because its founder, Patrick Colquhoun, like Peel before him, had a stake in colonial statecraft and the financial gains that accrued from it. Most police historians and criminologists know Colquhoun as the author of *A Treatise on the Police of the Metropolis*. What is lesser known and even more scantily reflected upon, however, is his involvement in 'develop[ing] a theory and practice of policing the industry' (Linebaugh, 2006: 409), by founding the River Thames Police in order to protect the profits that were amassed from the spoils of colonial plunder – like coffee, tea and sugar – which were 'the basis of the industrialization of England' (Linebaugh, 2006: 409). The Thames functioned as the 'jugular vein in the British Empire', connecting 'the workshops of Bengal, the plantations of the Caribbean, and the forests of North America' (Linebaugh, 2006: 409-10) and the River Thames Police was set up to accept 'direct responsibility for the payment of wages to lumping gangs of the West India fleet'

(Linebaugh, 2006: 433). As Linebaugh (2006: 410) stresses, '[t]hrough these waters passed the wealth of the Empire', and Colquhoun profited personally by working as 'the London agent for the planters of St. Vincent, Nevis, Dominica and the Virgin Islands' (Linebaugh, 2006: 426) – much like Peel acted as a colonial governor, managing the colonial occupation of Ireland.

Both Colquhoun and Peel, therefore, founded the two most influential British police forces, drawing on their experience as dutiful functionaries of the Empire. This otherwise obvious remark becomes important in any effort to expose the deceitfulness and dishonesty behind allusions to the ostensible political and ideological neutrality, or the benevolent purpose, of British policing. Conceived and instituted in the context of imperial-colonial rule, British policing could not be anything other than oppressive; destined, as it was, to protect the accumulation of capital that made industrial 'racial' capitalism' (Robinson, 2020)[5] possible at home and overseas. *This* was the rationale behind the foundation of policing, and its fate was inescapably tied to the expropriation of land and the exploitation of labour.

Such a journeying through the maritime *routes* of British colonialism through the slave trade and the violence that enabled it, is necessary for digging deep into the *roots* of British policing. However, this is not simply an exercise in time travel. It is an essential undertaking for understanding that when an institution, like policing, is instituted as an instrument of violence, its historical mission and function will not and cannot change – unless the violence it produces disappears and the activities and people it targets are no longer seen and policed as 'suspicious', 'dangerous' or 'threatening' to the status quo; imperial or postcolonial. This is why policing cannot and should not be thought of as a neutral or apolitical crime-fighting institution, and why the 'slightest familiarity with police history, or the sociology of policing' – as Loader (2020: 10) claims – is necessary as a bulwark against mistaken and misleading conceptions of policing. Just like policing was not founded with the aim to 'fight crime' – other than as an excuse – it continues to function as a tool for fighting against resistance to political power, as inscribed in law-making processes that legitimise and normalise unequal power relations (Fassin, 2013).

The argument here is that policing was – and remains – an instrument for the maintenance of social control, in the interests of an economic and political order that is also far from neutral, just, or democratic. Shocking though this assertion might seem, it would be inaccurate and irresponsible to claim that policing is fair or democratic when *only* the actions of *some* are targeted and only though the logics that serve *only* *some* people's interests; political, material or otherwise. Not everybody's activities and behaviours are seen and targeted as 'suspicious', 'risky', 'threatening' or 'dangerous'. Not everybody becomes 'police property' and not everybody decides what becomes 'law', or how we are ruled. With the Coronavirus regulations as a case in point, some legislation is not even discussed in parliament and can be unlawful too. Recent examples include the unlawful prorogation of parliament in the heyday of Brexit, the breaking of international law with the UK government's internal market bill, and the passing of COVID-19 regulations by ministerial decree; thereby bypassing parliamentary scrutiny. What all this points to is not a list of exceptions to the rule, but an illustration of how the creation of laws and policing deviate from 'democratic' procedures.

This is important, because the conceptual imagery of policing that we are socialised and educated into persists stubbornly as a 'piece of sturdy common-sense that is hard to gainsay' (Loader, 2020: 10). Yet, it must be challenged lest we forget that policing is – as Loader (2020: 11) argues – 'a site for the production of meaning and myth. It is an institution onto and through which people project various hopes and aspirations, fears and fantasies, about the social world'. Proceeding through aspirations, fears and fantasies, however, militates against any factually accurate, sensible and responsible understanding of the criminal justice – or rather criminal legal – institutions that we are ruled and policed by.

Beyond the long and complicated history of policing that we have caught a glimpse of so far, the very linguistic, political and ideological roots of 'the police' in most European languages and cultures also betray the political nature of policing (Knemeyer and Trib, 1980). In English, *police* shares its etymology with Latin and Greek words for governing (*politics*) the state (*polis*) through the administration (*policy*) and ordering (*policing*) of citizens (*polites*). This is why policing is approached in this book as an institution that exists to enforce discipline, to maintain control and to regulate order for the state – in ways that protect and preserve social rank and hierarchy, rather than bringing, maintaining or guaranteeing public safety. What constitutes a 'crime' and who and what is 'criminal'; what the law is or says; how the law is made; whom it protects; and how the state wields political power through policing – these are all intrinsically political matters. The very notion of 'crime' itself is actually 'the *product*' not the '*object*' of criminal justice policy (Hulsman, 1986: 71). It is 'a product of perception and political process' (Reiner, 2016: 6), which 'deems a certain "occurrence" or "situation" as undesirable [and] attributes that undesirable occurrence to an individual' (Hulsman, 1986: 71). As Nils Christie (1993: 21) has it: '[a]cts are not, they become. Crime does not exist. Crime is created. First there are acts. Then follows a long process of giving meaning to these acts. Distance increases the tendency to give certain acts the meaning of being crimes, and the persons the simplified meaning of criminals'.

'Crime', therefore, is not the social problem we think it is. It is also a problematic term. While it is typically understood as being a type of human behaviour, a distinct social phenomenon and a threat to public safety, a closer look at legal and criminological interpretations paints a more

POLICING 'THE PUBLIC' AS A VIRUS

complicated picture. While 'crime' is approached legally as an action or omission that constitutes an offence and is punishable by law, it should be understood as a process of definition – and making laws to reflect that definition. In other words, 'crime' is not a standalone act or a single social phenomenon, but a *reaction* to human behaviours and actions that are regarded as morally repugnant and socially harmful by those who have the power to define them as such. Seen in this way, 'crime' is better understood if it is placed within inverted commas and approached as a process that turns what are thought of as objectionable actions into legally punishable offences. It is therefore not a 'thing' – or just one 'thing' – and it is not always violent, though we often confuse it with, and mistake 'crime' for, the activities that the word describes. There are crimes that are not violent (for example, parking violations, fly-tipping), and there are violent acts that are not crimes (for example, wars, animal slaughter). Yet, we often think of violence when we think about crimes and make the two seem identical.

The difference between 'crimes' that are not violent and forms of violence that are not 'criminal', therefore, is *politics* – the power of making decisions and laws to purge acts, activities, behaviours, individuals and groups that are defined and pursued as 'criminal'. What policing does is to concentrate on 'activities [that are] potentially damaging to communal good order' (Neocleous, 2000: 4); but what is 'damaging', what is 'communal' and what constitutes 'good order' are fundamentally *political* questions, and the power of defining what those words mean does not rest with us all. Miles Ogborn's research on policing in Victorian England offers a vivid illustration of the historical dimension(s) that frame notions of 'good order':

> No longer were [the streets] to be a market place for farm animals, a theatre for public entertainments, a shop counter or an impromptu abattoir. Pavements and roads

were to be kept clear of all obstruction and dangers, from crowds and cattle to furniture and ferocious dogs. They were to be become arteries whose orderly flows of people and goods involved the rationalisation and regulation of the moral behaviour of the streets users. (Ogborn, 1993: 517)

In our time, this is not radically different from so-called 'public order' or 'quality of life' offences that criminalise people and activities through environmental control and the sanitisation of urban social life. In fact, the logic and the legislation that informs Public Spaces Protection Orders is based on the nearly 200-year-old Vagrancy Act, which came into force in 1824 and is still used to remove rough-sleeping and homeless people out of town centres. The 'vagrants' and 'loiterers' 'represented a mobile anomaly in the structure of social control' (Neocleous, 2000: 20) in Victorian England. Yet, the disorder they symbolised and *embodied* continues to be an 'offence' and is policed as such, through beat patrol ideologies that underpin mainstream notions of order, propriety and danger. This notion of danger, however, does not just occupy the minds of the police; it also shapes how policy makers, legislators, parliamentarians and some of their constituents think.

Fixing broken windows or (re)designing public safety?

Such punitive views of what public order is, or should be, and what the police should do to enforce it, became normalised, legitimised and mainstream following Kelling and Wilson's (1982) influential 'broken windows' theory (or, rather, broken windows 'theory').[6] Kelling and Wilson's (1982) hypothesis started its life as an op-ed in *The Atlantic*, but became a standard point of reference in academic and policy-making circles as a way of seeing. It is an ideology of 'crime' through an imagery of social disorder that plagues 'the law-abiding', because brazen interlopers trespass within the public domain, when they should (ideally) remain out of sight, if not locked up. Approaching 'crime' as the symptom of disorder – caused by the lingering presence of 'vagrants' – is the central tenet of Kelling and Wilson's aggressive musings on public safety.

Simplistic though such a self-serving platitude is, it nevertheless won the hearts and minds of political parties and police departments – to say nothing of the proverbial 'law-abiding' citizen. As such, 'broken windows' policing rose to the ranks of state ideology and policy mantra that drew its strength from lurid depictions of 'obstreperous teenager[s]' or 'drunken panhandler[s]', who ostensibly haunt the life and experience of the city as 'fear-inducing' spectres in the hawkish imagination of Kelling and Wilson (1982) and their devotees. According to such paranoid 'criminal' symptomatology, '[t]he unchecked panhandler is, in effect, the first broken window', which signals 'disorderly behavior' and spirals into '[s]erious street crime' that 'flourishes' in areas that are populated by such undesirable defilers of public space and public order.

The idea that nuisance might be irritating, inconvenient even, but hardly the root of all evil that Kelling and Wilson make it out to be – is wasted on them. Nor do they pause to think about the implications of their disciplinarian thinking on the human and political rights of those who are seen *only* as a problem to be solved. Consequently, the notion of 'improving places' through funding public social infrastructures of care and support, rather than 'punishing people' (Klinenberg, 2018: 59), never plays a part in their work. That would certainly be a waste of public funds on people who are seen *as* waste – which explains why this model has the ears of police chiefs and politicians who would rather fund policing, than invest in public infrastructure.

If this reminds anyone of the 'authoritarian populism' (Hall, 1979) of Thatcher and Reagan, this is because that is the doctrine that dictates Kelling and Wilson's politics. For them, like Thatcher and Reagan before them, policing – instead of providing and caring – should be the order of the day; achieved through 'slashing the social wage by cutting welfare benefits, public education, and public housing, and smashing public and private unions, all the while lowering taxes on the rich and on corporations and increasing spending on military, police, and prisons' (Gilmore and Gilmore, in Camp and Heatherton, 2016: 173).

Since 'order maintenance' means doling out 'quality of life' offences through 'broken windows' policing, the targets of policing become defined through a language, rhetoric and logic that bring 'the habits of the poor into the jurisdiction of the police' (Williams, 2015: 128). The example of how public space is policed as a site of disorder at the expense of 'good order' helpfully illustrates that what counts as, and what becomes, 'criminal' is not *the product of people's behaviours*, but *the outcome of political decisions*. Simply put, '[t]he modern police system was designed to keep the marginalized in their place and to warn the poor of a fate worse than poverty' (Platt, 2015) – and that is what it continues to do today. The police do not target or pursue the Health Secretary for acting 'unlawfully' by breaching 'the "vital public function" of transparency over how "vast quantities" of taxpayers' money was spent' (Conn, 2021). Equally, they do not step in to protect 'the public' from the Home Secretary's detention policies, which breached human rights rules (Taylor, 2021).

These examples are not even recognised or read as 'crimes', or as acts of violence that pose a threat and a danger to the integrity of the law or indeed to the preservation of 'good order'. They may be 'unlawful' acts that 'breach the law', but they are certainly not crimes, nor are government ministers criminals. Laws against such ministerial (mis)conduct obviously exist and are obviously broken, but the police do not spend their energy on pursuing the minor wrongdoings or misdemeanours of government ministers. Yet, the police *do* direct their attention to the minor wrongdoings or misdemeanours of those who drink publicly, loiter or sleep rough – because these *are* crimes, not just 'unlawful' acts or mere 'breaches' of the law.

Such an observation might seem unkind or ungenerous to notions of legality, yet even liberal-minded thinkers like the 'Father of Liberalism', John Locke, openly recognise that political power, law making and the allocation of rights according to property are inseparable. In fact, Locke learned all that from his personal experience as a senior administrator of slave-owning colonies and as a writer, not of learned treatises alone, but of slave codes too (Fryer, 1993, 29; Linebaugh, 2006: 52–3). Locke is therefore mentioned here, as a figure who embodies the approach to policing that this book adopts: as a political instrument, whose function is dictated by its history as an institution that was created to protect the interests of property and to crush any resistance by those who dared to escape their fate as property.

Thinking about Locke as someone who 'played a large role in the creation of the Board of Trade; the architect of the old colonial system' (Fryer, 1993: 29) is interesting as a way of impersonating the ideological and historical forces that created policing. Policing then becomes understood as an institution that upholds and services the colonial-imperial order that Locke helped to shape by 'draft[ing] instructions to the governor of Virginia [then a British colony] in which black slavery was justified', or indeed by writing the constitution of Barbados based on slave codes 'enacting that human beings become "real chattels"' (Linebaugh, 2006: 52).

Our discussion of policing as a political institution, whose current form bears the imprint of its imperial-colonial history, should therefore serve as a reminder that the politics *of* – as well as *in* – policing also derive from that same history. Who and what *is* property, why property should determine one's social status and treatment by laws that are drafted to protect property and those with property, are political and historical facts. As is the fact that policing was conceived and evolved as the very institution that is charged with protecting this state of affairs. Yet, the mythology of British policing as a fair, impartial institution, imbued with democratic, egalitarian and ethical principles of justice and organised around consent, endures.

This is often couched in language that extols the virtues of 'policing by consent' as a cornerstone of British policing and indeed as the very principle that Robert Peel grafted onto policing. But it is a myth. Indeed the so-called 'Peelian principles' that are supposed to inform a time-honoured tradition of 'policing by consent' are neither Peelian nor consensual. As Clive Emsley (2013) points out, there is little evidence to show that the Peelian principles were actually written by Peel. Instead they are thought of as the brainchild of Charles Reith, author of *A Short History of the British Police* and *British Police and the Democratic Ideal*.

As for 'policing by consent', it rests on the – naive at best, insulting at worst – idea that we consent to being policed, even though policing entails the threat of force. This Home Office picture of policing[7] – which romantically appeals to a revered Victorian colonial administrator and founder of the Conservative Party (Robert Peel) – would have us believe that we apparently *can* and *do* consent to being policed, even under the threat of force. We therefore consent, despite the fact that we are coerced into consenting, knowing that the police can use force to assert dominance and exert authority. In reality, consent is *produced* by and through affluent, white populations who have little or no contact with the police.

For the people who are policed, there is only force. In fact, this is not even a secret or anything that the police would care to conceal or feel embarrassed by. Some even proudly declare it publicly, as illustrated by a tweet from Steve James, the Gloucestershire Police Federation Chairman, who lays bare the priorities of the police. Writing in the aftermath of protests against police violence against women and against the UK government's Policing, Crime, Sentencing and Courts Bill, James tweeted (on 27 March 2021 at 12:49am) that '[p]olicing by consent is a general principle not duty', adding that 'technically we're crown servants not public servants'. Even high-ranking police officials themselves expose the democratic idea(l) of policing for the deceitful conceit that it is.

So, if consent is not a duty and the police actually serve the Crown, then the responsibility of the police is not to 'us', 'the public', but to the state and its monarch Queen Elizabeth II. 'Policing by consent', therefore, is a mythological and much mythologised story that poses as the foundation for a system of beliefs about policing that soothe white middle-class people – whose faith in the police is rooted in the certainty that they (would) consent to being policed, were they to have much contact with the police as suspects in the first place. These populations tend to consider policing as natural, normal and inevitable, because they are not imagined, talked about, personified or processed as 'police property'.[8] Yet, there seems to be no moral or legal obligation even to such a 'respectable', 'law-abiding', tax-paying 'public' as far as the police are concerned. Instead, as the Gloucestershire Police Federation Chairman reminds us, they (only) swear allegiance to the Crown.

Beyond hashtag chatter, however, police helmets also tell us as much. Think of the bejewelled crown adorning officers' headgear, which is also omnipresent in police badges too. What else could the presence of a crown symbolise other than faith in, and obedience to, the Crown? Well, it symbolises – that is to say, represents – a story about the institution of policing and the political history of Britain too as imperial-colonial. Since we cannot have a Crown without (the) Royals and there can be no Royals without an Empire, it is also impossible to have an Empire without colonies. Likewise, it is impossible to have colonies without expropriating land and exploiting people by turning them into colonial property. And it would be patently absurd to glorify the Empire without embracing its violent history as a brutal regime that relied on slave trade for its riches, as it relied on colonial militias and police forces for enforcing that imperial-colonial order 'out there' in the colonies, and 'right here' in the metropole.

With such history rooted in imperial-colonial domination which is enthusiastically celebrated, but with the bad bits conveniently left out – any allusions to democracy or consent are insulting. The very ideology of British policing since its inception has been based on a colonial logic, whether this plays out at home or overseas. Thomas Carlyle's chilling description of how the public ought to consent to being subjected to force is rather fitting here:

> Bellowings, inarticulate cries as of a dumb creature in rage and pain; to the ear of wisdom they are inarticulate prayers: 'Guide me, govern me! I am mad, and miserable, and cannot guide myself!' Surely of all 'rights of man', this right of the ignorant man to be guided by the wiser, to be gently or forcibly, held in the true course by him, is the indisputablest. (Carlyle, 1998: 161)

These words were penned as a response to the Chartists' protests for parliamentary reform in support of the working class in England, but they express the same logic that was employed to justify colonialism overseas – as a civilising mission: an expedition designed to bring civilisation through violence, brutal force and coercion. The idea of the police as what Storch (1993) referred to as 'domestic missionaries', also rests on a colonial ideology of policing as a civilising mission at home. After all, this is what the notion of the 'thin blue line' embodies; with the police forming that 'blue' line of defence that protects 'civilisation' from a descent into barbarism (Wall, 2020). Just as the threat of slave rebellions and insurrections created militias to repress such activity, the activities of the 'dangerous' working classes brought the activities of the poor, the marginalised and those who are racialised as non-white in contact with the violent arm of the state: the police.

That is the story that this chapter wants to tell about policing, so we can wake up and face up to its history, to better understand its current function. Unless, of course, we think that the way that an institution is historically constituted is irrelevant to how it operates today – even though it draws on the *same* logics, the *same* laws and the *same* people to police against the same populations that are labelled as dangerous and threatening to an unequal social order that depends on inequality and social hierarchy for its survival.

In direct confrontation to state and police ideologies that see, target, monitor, pursue, arrest, sentence and imprison people as dangerous, this chapter – and this book on the whole – argue the exact opposite. What is seen as a public threat is policing itself. As such, it serves, protects and enforces an unequal social, economic and political order that is founded on historical processes of extraction, subjugation and exploitation that endure to this day. The type of economy and political governance that we currently have is capitalism and it is racial by default, since capitalism requires hierarchies, and logics of racial ordering provide them.

In the context of COVID-19, the critique that we have offered about policing as an expression of state power and organised violence is relevant to the fact that being policed does not mean being protected from the virus. It simply means being policed as the virus. As we noted at the beginning of this chapter, none of this criticism is meant as a suggestion that emergency laws should not be observed when this is all we have – in the absence of a proper public infrastructure of care. However, this does not absolve us of our responsibility to reflect on the policing of COVID-19 as a way of understanding what policing is and what it does. Thinking about the new police powers that the Coronavirus legislation granted, and relating such expanded powers to the arguments that this chapter has proposed, allows us to question whether policing is based on democratic legitimacy rather than repressive authority.

Given that such police powers are arbitrary in their design and unrestrained in their force, this should raise urgent questions about who is more likely to be targeted under such legislation, on what grounds, and based on whose interpretation of such laws. For example, whatever may count as 'reasonable excuse' or 'reasonable force' in the Health Protection (Coronavirus, Restrictions) (England) Regulations 2020, largely relies on police officers' individual judgement, who often rely on guidance rather than the law itself. For example, in the original formulation of the Coronavirus regulations there was *no* explicit prohibition on leaving one's home *only* once a day, there was *no* time limit by which one had to return home, and there was *no* requirement that one may leave one's home only for exceptional reasons. Enforcing such vague regulations, therefore, ultimately results in their arbitrary application by officers who are given wider powers of discretion to decide what restrictions are breached and what charges are to be made.

This is made worse by the realisation that these regulations convert almost all 'normal' social behaviour into anti-social behaviour, thereby turning fundamental rights and civil liberties (such as freedom of movement and freedom of assembly) into criminal offences. Some might, and indeed will, dismiss such concerns as little more than liberal hand-wringing. However, in the light of the two-year time span of the Coronavirus Bill (later, Act) and the lack of parliamentary scrutiny or approval of the Coronavirus regulations, concerns about civil liberties are far from exaggerated or unfounded. Such warnings serve to nurture attentiveness to what happens when arbitrary state power is increased, with policing at the forefront.

In order to conclude, it is worth returning to the key messages of this chapter. The policing of COVID-19 and 'the public' as a virus laid bare the function, operations and logic of the state as a form of 'political authority', which 'serve[s] to orchestrate and to some degree mystify the structure of economic relations' (Robinson, 2016: 160). Seen this way, the state no longer stands in for a political (infra)structure that is designed with mutualist, solidaristic and welfarist idea(ls) in mind. It is a network of institutions where wealth (money) and power (ability to control) accumulate and need a force (police) for their protection through coercion. As Tilly (1992: 19) succinctly puts it, 'when the accumulation [of capital] and concentration of [political power and] coercive means grow together, they produce states'. Or, as Gordon Clark and Michael Dear argue, 'we conceive of the state as deriving equally from the economic and political imperatives of capitalist commodity production. The state is ultimately implicated in the generation and distribution of surplus value as it seeks to sustain its own power and wealth' (Clark and Dear in Tilly, 1992: 10).

If the state is linked to capital as its material lifeline and power source, how is that capital made? The answer is to be found in the history of imperial-colonial rule, whose roots are tangled up with the *routes* of the transatlantic slave trade and slavery as a political regime of racial governance. As for policing, it emerged as a political virus; a disease that spreads its harmful and corrupting influence through the use of state-sanctioned violence and force, to maintain a capitalist order that is shaped by, and based on, hierarchies of 'race', class, gender and sexuality – as terms of exclusion that create targets for violence.

Reading policing as the servant of an unequal political order that creates inequalities through social division along lines of 'difference', has therefore meant understanding how and why all policing is shot through with hierarchies of power that policing serves, protects and maintains. This being the political order that enlists policing as a coercive, violent state institution with which to respond to social problems or public health emergencies, such public health emergencies become public order issues. And when the police roam the streets in search of 'crimes' to create and 'criminals' to pursue by identifying – nay, profiling them – as such, what the police do is to enforce an order that is based on hierarchies of racial, material and political power.

In light of all this, it is therefore vital to recognise that some are violently policed in order to 'protect' – to protect capital and white supremacy that is. The myth of a democratic 'thin blue line' that keeps brutality in check therefore has no chance of surviving, if we think and politically organise in ways that expose policing as the state's order maintenance institution that cuts across the class and colour line and produces violence that is at once classed, 'raced' and heteronormatively gendered.

TWO

The order of public health

In this chapter, we explore the intimate relationship between 'public health' and 'public order', arguing that understanding them together allows us to understand ways in which states may intensify their interventions and expand their power with little regard for democratic accountability. What connects them is the question of 'the public'. With public order, the spectre of the 'disorderly' is presented as a problem that must be contained and policed against. In public health, disease, ill-health and contagion are also staged as something that needs to be 'fought'. The argument here is that disorder and disease have been historically linked not only in terms of who is considered a threat to the order and the health of the state, but also in terms of the state performing its assumed necessity for social life by 'fighting' disorder and disease.

In light of this, this chapter asks how the language of conflict and war is utilised to stage political responses that foreground 'order' to medical threats to the state that are simultaneously presented as issues of 'health'. We investigate the manner in which the 'health' of the state is predicated on an idea of order that is to be secured via the police. It will be shown that what is deemed disorderly is linked to disease and ill-health; and furthermore that this, far from being a recent phenomenon, has a very long history in Western political thought and political practice. In this way, the pandemic, and the political response to it, will be revealed as being framed by a conception of the body politic where order, safety and health are linked to the suppression of disorder and disease via police.

In a variety of ways, and through manifold means, we are relentlessly given the message that without money and without government – indeed without *police* – society would break down, civil war would erupt, and chaos and catastrophe would ensue. It helps to remind ourselves of the political history of this idea, because it enables us to remember that these ideas are not natural or inevitable, but rather the consequence of a long conceptual and political–institutional history. This history has, for various reasons, been constructed and reproduced to the extent that we forget they were made, and to the extent that we forget that things could be *otherwise*. As Mariame Kaba writes, 'it is not simply that we can't imagine a world without police, but that we are disciplined into not having that imagination' (Kaba, 2020).

This chapter begins by trying to unearth some of those moments where that disciplining takes place through key metaphors, analogies, languages and epistemologies. We show that the health of the state and our individual health have become tied together through a series of interventions and practices that reproduce anti-Black and racist logics.

Policing the body politic

'We need you Boris, your health is the health of the nation' (Pearson, 2020)

When UK Prime Minister Boris Johnson fell ill with COVID-19 in April 2020, journalists and political commentators were quick to associate his individual health with the health of the state, as well as denouncing those who sought to point out his own folly regarding the virus. After initially downplaying the virus against mounting evidence that serious and immediate action needed to be taken, he had now contracted the virus himself and had to be hospitalised in intensive care as a result. As this *Telegraph* headline encapsulates, that the Prime Minister had become infected seemed to pose a threat beyond his health as an individual. But a threat to what? Or, rather, to whom? Something more was clearly at stake here – and that something can be explained via the notion of the 'body politic'.

While a full explanatory history of this curious rhetorical device is not within the scope of this book, its resurgent relevance for comprehending the state reaction to the pandemic – and, in turn, some people's reactions to the state – makes a discussion of it necessary. It is an ancient metaphor, one that likens political communities to human bodies, with different agencies of state being likened to different body parts, as well as providing a sense in which the whole of the political body is bigger than the sum of its parts. The metaphor highlights concerns with harmony, health and longevity; seeing political life as needing certain conditions in order to survive. Though hugely important for the conceptualisation of the state, the metaphor had somewhat taken a backseat in recent decades, becoming increasingly associated with the 'wrong' kind of state – one where the whole was more important than the part, where individuals served the common community, and indeed where individuals can be *sacrificed* for the good of the whole. In short, it conjured images of totalitarianism, authoritarianism and fascism, to which liberal democracies were distinctly opposed. Marin Terpstra identifies roughly three different uses of the body politic analogy that are supposedly anathema to democracies:

> Roughly speaking, the political body had been used in three ways, all of which are narrowly linked to monarchy: (1) as a normative model of a social and political order, in which the king is the head (and therefore also part of the political body); (2) as the body of the person representing the political community, in which the king

embodies the community; and (3) as an object of care and management, in which the king acts as a physician (coming from the outside) to protect the political body from illness and to guard its health. In a democracy, which means essentially the self-government of the people by the people, the idea of the political body can no longer be used in any of these ways; it may even lose its meaning and importance altogether. In this transformation, it becomes difficult to see the image of 'political body' as anything other than merely a product of imagination. (Terpstra, 2020: 46)

Though different iterations exist, generally in the political philosophy of liberalism, the individual exists prior to the state, and individuals come together to form states in order to be protected *as* individuals. These individuals are atomised market actors, who are rational, rights-bearing agents and, in this narrative, the state mostly exists to protect individual rights and freedoms,[1] not least individual rights and freedoms to earn money and buy property. 'Political society', C.B. Macpherson writes, 'becomes a calculated device for the protection of property and for the maintenance of an orderly relation of exchange' (Macpherson, 2011: 3).

A closer look at the idea of the body politic, however, reveals a concept not necessarily at odds with liberal philosophy and its ideas of state. That states became increasingly concerned with the biological status of their citizens throughout the 18th and 19th centuries has been well documented. Yet the idea that a healthy population should be a cornerstone of government is much older: 'the health of the people should be the supreme law' is a maxim found in Roman law and later repeated by the modern political thinkers such as Hobbes and Locke. This is the idea that the fundamental or overarching principle of government should be to protect and maintain the 'health' of the people. When paired with the body politic, however, we can see how the health of the people and the health of the state become essentially synonymous. That is, the health of the people is dependent on the state being 'healthy' and vice versa. If what constitutes healthy people seems somewhat self-evident (though this is not as straightforward as first appears, as we shall see later in this chapter), ideas of what constitutes a 'healthy state' are more contested.

The modern state is transformed by ideas of the social contract, where a reciprocal relationship is instituted: the state has a duty to protect its citizens, and for their part, the citizens have a duty to obey. Where the health of the people is the supreme law, this 'protection' consists of protection against threats to the state, which may be biological or viral but can equally be political, violent or seditious; in short, the threat of *disorder* that states claim to be the only imaginable bulwark against. Part of the task at hand, then, is to recover these points, not as an end in itself, but to remind ourselves that these things are not 'natural' or inevitable.

What does a 'healthy' state then look like? Even before the rise of liberalism and political economy, we find the health of the state tied to its financial status. For Hobbes and others, the 'blood' of the body politic is money:[2]

> Thomas Hobbes understood money as the blood in Leviathan's body, and the metaphor served pro-slavery Southerner John C. Calhoun equally well nearly two hundred years later. 'The currency of a country is to the community' Calhoun wrote in 1837, 'what the blood is to the body ... indispensable to all the functions of life'. (O'Malley, 1994: 372)

In the crucible of the modern state, the body politic is thus something that 'lives' because of two things: the sovereign, without which the 'people' do not exist; and money, which circulates around the body, giving life to its different parts. These beginnings are significant, in that they point to the ideas that have shaped and prefigured the present: without sovereignty, police and (the circulation of) money, the body politic ceases to exist. In Hobbes' rendering of the issue, we would then be at war with each other, a dissolved multitude no longer protected from the violence that each may use in self-defence, no longer able to make contracts which ensure our property. It is here that the 'war of all against all' begins.

While some would point out the hyperbolic tone of this account, it bears repeating that this is now political common sense – a predominant presupposition that our health is dependent on the health of the state; and the health of the state cannot be maintained without government, police and a 'healthy economy'. This barbed logic can be found at the centre of the US's and the UK's approach to the Coronavirus, where 'the economy' has been repeatedly invoked as a rationale for refusing to lock down or for pursuing 'herd immunity' (without a vaccine), for easing lockdown restrictions as cases were rising, for imploring people to get 'back to work', for opening schools, the list goes on. There was a choice to be made, we were told both more and less explicitly, between protecting the 'health of the state' (economy) and the health of individuals. Thus, what would then go on to lead to the US and the UK having two of the highest death rates in the world initially, was presented as public health policy. As Mitropoulos writes:

> indeed, the misnamed 'herd immunity' strategy would, despite the government's claims of protecting the vulnerable, actively enable the virus to cut a predictable path of destruction through existing patterns of private household wealth, ill-health and mortality exacerbated by decades of neoliberal policy – and call it a natural disaster. (Mitropoulos, 2020a: 57)

What we see again and again is political decisions being made that imperil people's health, particularly migrant workers, workers in low-paid, public-facing jobs, those who cannot 'work from home' in the name of the economy. Rishi Sunak's

'Eat Out to Help Out'[3] is but one of the most visible examples. If there was ever any doubt as to whether we serve the economy or the economy serves us, the pandemic has shown, for many, that the abstract realm known as 'the economy' has 'needs' that are repeatedly prioritised over the health, safety and lives of many. We have seen both rampant punitiveness, criminalisation and law and order politics from the government in response to the crisis, alongside and intersecting with a soft-touch 'economy first' approach.

Far from a contradiction, however, this is orthodox neoliberal doctrine.[4] The neoliberal project defined itself as distinct from the liberal project via a mantra of 'strong state, free economy' (Cristi, 1998). That is, a free market would not spontaneously or inevitably persist, but must be backed up with a 'strong state'. Thus, in England and coming from the same government, we see both Eat Out to Help Out and, conversely, 10-year prison sentences for holidaymakers who lie on travel forms. We see 70,000 fixed penalty notices given, including fines for walking on a beach (NPCC, 2021), as well as Boris Johnson launching a 'back to work campaign' despite rising numbers of cases (Rayner, 2020). What, however, does a 'strong state' consist of?

Adriana Cavarero has argued that as far back as the ancient Greeks, we find an exchange between medicine and politics, where order, health and hierarchy are considered synonymous, and where 'any disturbance of hierarchy is considered a disease' (Cavarero, 2002: 103). The body politic, as a body, must be protected against ill-health and disease both literally and metaphorically. We see this at work in Plato's Republic which recounts Socrates as declaring that when a person is unhealthy, 'the addition of a touch from without may bring on illness, and sometimes even when there is no external provocation a commotion may arise within – in the same way wherever there is weakness in the State there is also likely to be illness, of which the occasions may be very slight … and then the State falls sick and is at war with herself' (Plato, 1994).

What we can begin to see here are the very deep roots of an idea that likens the state to a body that is vulnerable to sickness, where health has been associated with good order, and where disease and disorder are made to appear as sicknesses that may occur from without or within the borders of the state. Clues to the conceptual and historical linkage of health and order are littered throughout the history of the modern state. Take, for example, Thomas Hobbes' *Leviathan* (1996). Widely regarded as a forefather of modern Western statecraft, Hobbes' theories help to illuminate the grounds on which the state imaginary has been constructed. One does not even have to open the book to find, on the frontispiece, an empty city containing a scattering of tiny figures. The city does not contain the people who are to be found in the body of the King, but only plague doctors and security guards.[5] The history of policing and public health tells us that this, far from being metaphorical, attests to an actual institutional and practical mutual dependence between them.

This is useful for thinking through the current situation, in that it helps to shed light on the deep conceptual *and* institutional histories of public order and public health. It helps us to understand the state response to the pandemic and the immediate reach for police and public order as a solution. In other words, in the state's imagination, health cannot be conceived of outside of order, or outside of the *policing* of order. Though there are important differences between, say, the Ancient Greek rendering of the body politic, and later medieval notions and modern ones, what is significant here is that the state has been configured as a body, with different institutions comprising different anatomical parts – the sovereign has been thought of as the 'head' or the 'soul', the police as the 'hands', money as blood circulating throughout the polity. It is important to note here that the state is conceived of as a 'whole', with different parts that operate in order to keep the whole alive. The analogies change, different body parts are likened to different institutions, but the legacy of such political thought is the idea that the state is a unified whole that must be defended against certain threats – be those biological, environmental or political.

Health police?

That the health of the population became an increasingly prominent concern of Western states throughout the 18th and 19th centuries is now something of a truism, not least due to the work of Foucault and his interlocutors. Indeed, it was in what was known as the 'police-state' that the notion that the safety, welfare and health of the population as a whole should not be left to chance, but must be actively *promoted* and *regulated* by government agencies and policies. This was the job originally assigned to 'police'.[6] Most scholarship on the police presents the concept as being split between a premodern notion and a modern one. The word 'police' was not officially used in Great Britain until 1714, referring then to the ten 'Commissioners of Police' in Scotland (Oxford English Dictionary, 1989). Prior to this, the corresponding concept had already begun to take shape on the continent, in particular in Germany and France in the 15th century, eventually giving rise to a form of governing that was the 'legislative and administrative regulation of the internal life of a community to promote general welfare and the condition of good order ... and the regimenting of social life' (Neocleous, 2000: 1).

At this time, police meant something similar to 'policy'; directing and managing people who lived in a particular jurisdiction. As Foucault tells us, this 'premodern' police see to a broad range of things, including: religion, health, morals, public safety, liberal arts, trade, the poor; in other words, he finds that in most treatises on police in the 17th and 18th centuries, the 'police see to everything' (Foucault, 1979: 249).

For Foucault, this is a turning point in the history of state power, which is no longer exercised in pursuit of wider ethical or virtuous goals, but rather to secure and maintain its power in a hostile/competitive international arena. In *The Political Technology of Individuals*, Foucault tells us that: 'It [police] wields its power over living beings as living beings, and its politics therefore has to be a biopolitics' (Foucault, 2002: 416). Biopolitics, Foucault writes elsewhere, 'deals with the population, with the population as a political problem, as a problem that is at once scientific and political, as a biological problem and as power's problem' (Foucault, 2004: 245). In this latter account, individuals were henceforth seen in their capacity as increasing the power of the state, and so the state must concern itself with the vitality and health of the population at large. The 'police' project is from the beginning simultaneously and predominantly then a 'public health' project and this, in turn, is the project of ensuring the increased power and wealth of the sovereign state.

This 'premodern' concept of police was intrinsically tied to health via sanitation regulations, the rise in public hygiene and other state practices, laws and policies aimed at keeping the state 'clean' and 'healthy'. This is perhaps best summed up via the architect of this so-called 'medical police', Johann Peter Frank. Frank, a German doctor and hygienist, held prominent positions at various universities, before being appointed by the emperor of Austria to the position of director of public health. Throughout the 1700s, Frank published six volumes of his 'System of Medical Police'. The state, as Frank conceived of it, had a duty to enforce health regulations, as well as monitoring and regulating the health of the population as a whole. Not to be confused with clinical medicine, the rise of medical police 'focuses more explicitly on population's *vital* dimensions (public health, occupational safety, food, sanitation, dwellings, disposal of corpses, regulation of health practitioners, elimination of quacks, building of hospitals, and marriage and procreation, including all the vicissitudes thereof: fertility, sterility, prostitution, unwed mothers, masturbation etc.)' (Cohen, 2009: 97). As the name 'medical police' suggests, this form of governing was seen as one that required *force*. In Frank's own words:

> medical police, like all police science, is an art of defense, a model of protection of people and their animal helpers against the deleterious consequences of dwelling together in large numbers, but especially of promoting their physical well-being so that the people will succumb as late as possible to their eventual fate from the many physical illnesses to which they are subject. (Frank, 1976: 12)

Over the course of the 18th century and into the 19th century, it is thought that the concept of police began to undergo a series of shifts in meaning; in particular, what was once a broad, all-encompassing police power becomes limited and narrowed. So, on the one hand, there is a continental notion of police, originating in France and Germany, concerned with order, peace, and the happiness of its citizens (Tribe, 1995: 12). In other words, contained within the concept of police was the notion of a *public good* that meant health, happiness and security. On the other hand, we find a later, more modern, notion of police as a 'regular uniform patrol of public space coupled with *post hoc* investigation of reported or discovered crime or disorder' (Reiner, 2010: 5). It is argued that this is the result of a 'struggle over the function of the police and the *restriction* of their activities' (Knemeyer and Trib, 1980: 186, emphasis added).

For many who trace the lineage and history of 'police', the rise of liberalism and political economy necessitated the restriction of police power, a narrowing of its function to the 'elimination of disorder' (Foucault, 2007: 354) and an 'apparatus or instrument for ensuring the prevention or repression of disorder, irregularity, illegality and delinquency' (Foucault, 2007: 353). These are 'simply negative functions'; and, furthermore, police will simply be the 'instrument by which one prevents the occurrence of certain disorders'

(Foucault, 2007: 354). Police, in other words, becomes a negative power, in direct opposition to its previous incarnation as a positive one.[7] It is supposedly with this transformation of police power, from an incredibly wide regulatory power, to one concerned with preventing and detecting crime, that the police we now see around us takes shape:

> So it was in the early 19th century that this transformation took place, for, as noted, the function attributed to the police would from that point onward, be significantly whittled down from that of economic police to that of a security police, an institutional tool devoted to the sole task of managing the risks and dangers incident to the unhindered unfolding of spontaneous socioeconomic processes. (Campesi, 2016: 200)

With economic transformation and the move to a capitalist economic system – as well as the linked process of a shift in governance to individual rights, liberalism and formal democracy – police power, it has been said, needed to be cut back, to allow for the spontaneous processes of economic liberalism to take root, and for individuals to have their private sphere of freedom protected. The state, in other words, needed to be expelled from the marketplace as well as the home, and individual freedoms to 'truck, barter and exchange' needed to take precedence. Put simply, police, it is said, can no longer be concerned with regulating behaviour, conduct, morals, health or trade, but are simply there to uphold and enforce the law. As Campesi argues: 'We could say that police would never again be understood as the highest expression of a ... power of the sovereign authority to promote the public welfare – and would henceforth be reduced to a[n] ... activity concerned with averting future ills' (Campesi, 2016: 200).

In the late 18th into the 19th centuries, these transformations in state and economy were seen by Foucault as inaugurating a distinctly new form of power: biopolitics. David Tarizzo, describing Foucault's thought on this shift, says:

> During the 1970s, Foucault will in fact argue that in the Modern Age a new form of power spreads, one that is detached from the law of the sword, from the classical code of sovereignty, in order to take charge of life as such. Its motto is no longer Take life or let live but Make live and let die (Foucault 1978). Power, that is, now targets life itself, a life to be cultivated, empowered, directed, and regulated. (Tarizzo, 2017: 19)

Many scholars have used Foucault's framework for understanding modern power to grasp the political landscape shaped by the pandemic. What we have witnessed in the past months has been seen by many as the mobilisation of a huge biopolitical apparatus, one concerned with life itself: 'making live and letting die'. The prospect of 'immunity passports', whereby individuals will be able to travel based on a record of their vaccinations and antibodies in their blood seems the latest ongoing attempt to securitise health – and indeed an added factor to the expanding surveillance state and biometric security operations, where one's *individual* health is subject to state management and surveillance.

Yet, the ongoing pandemic, and the policing of it, must also be seen as a manifestation of that which had supposedly been lost with the ascent of biopolitics and the liberal state. That is to say, this is not simply the triumph of a distinctly modern form of power that Foucault identifies, but also the perseverance of the 'premodern' police power: where the public welfare means managing and implementing public health and public order measures, and where the function of policing becomes as vague and far-reaching as the laws and regulations they supposedly implement. Perhaps, then, the pandemic has forged order and health back together in a new way, demonstrating a resurgence of an old form of power that many thought had been lost sometime in the 19th century. Perhaps. Yet we could also surmise that this form of power was never 'lost' to begin with, that when police are charged with creating and maintaining 'order', the word 'order' must be seen as containing multitudes – multitudes that by no means exclusively, but largely, map on to those functions that 'premodern' police were seen to have. In short, when we say that police maintain or uphold 'order', we find that what 'order' is cannot be defined in advance, but rather points to any number of activities police can or could undertake, thus belying the sense in which modern policing is simply negative, reactive or limited.[8]

The pandemic has challenged the view that sees police power as having been transformed in the 19th century, no longer with a concern to 'promote the public welfare' and indeed the prevailing view that modern policing has little to do with premodern policing. The policing of the pandemic makes little sense without a longer historical view that sees the function of policing as being concerned with both the 'health' and 'order' of the state and its citizens. The Coronavirus Act was fast-tracked and passed through parliament in a day in March 2020. The Act greatly extends executive powers, including giving powers to the police to detain and isolate people who are 'potentially infectious', as well as empowering the executive to close borders and ban public gatherings and protests. Coming under the banner of emergency legislation, over 70 Coronavirus regulations came into force before being debated by parliament (Liberty, 2020). The then Health Secretary, Matt Hancock, justified the enormity and fast pace of this Act, telling parliament: 'The measures that I have outlined are unprecedented in peacetime. We will fight this virus with everything we have. We are in a war with an invisible killer and we have to do everything we can to stop it' (quoted in Musu, 2020).

The language of conflict and war has saturated political and medical rhetoric on COVID-19. Yet this language also constitutes the history of the language of 'immunity' *as such* since the 1880s (Cohen, 2009: 3). The notion that one can 'fight' a disease, and where one's immune system is seen as a 'defence', is now so commonplace that we forget that this language is not self-evident, but the result of a cross-pollination between political and medical lexicon that ends up being presented as fact. As Cohen writes of the emergence of medical discourse around immunity: 'it imagines the individual organism as the space within which a cellular struggle for survival (a.k.a. disease) takes place, and conversely defines a specific microbial agent as the hostile cause against which the organism must wage its relentless war with death' (Cohen, 2009: 5).

This way of picturing individual organisms is very close to a Hobbesian 'state of nature', where self-defence – and indeed the use of violence for self-defence – is the fundamental 'right of nature', which he characterises as 'by all means we can, to defend our selves' (Hobbes, 1996: 91). Self-defence, and the use of force or violence in that defence, is figured as a 'law of nature' or natural law that, after the creation of government, is transferred to the sovereign. This means that after a government is formed, we give up our right to 'defend' ourselves, and collectively relinquish that power to the sovereign, who defends us as a collective. This extremely powerful idea is still with us today. The state, as discussed in Chapter One, has a monopoly on violence, which is to say the state *and only* state-sanctioned people, can use violence.[9] Police officers are permitted to use violence to defend 'the common good', but if you or I did, it would be a criminal offence. Armies are deployed to use violence to 'defend' the home country. Anything else is terrorism: *de facto* illegitimate, because not state sanctioned. The state, in this narrative, is thus not only positioned as having a monopoly on violence, but is also – and crucially – positioned *precariously*. Disease and disorder threaten the state both from without and from within. Foreign armies and foreign diseases, as well as criminals, rebels and dissidents, all constitute potential threats, which the government must defend against.

There is a crucial slippage in this latter narrative that we would do well to take note of. Threats *to the state* are positioned as threats to everyone *within* the state. This is where the exchange between medicine and politics can be seen in its full significance, because it is in this slippage that our individual lives are cast as being tied to the continuation of the state. It is here that the 'disorderly', positioned as being a threat to the state, becomes synonymous with foreign armies and with plagues. The disease of disorder cannot come from the sovereign or government, because they are, by definition, the antithesis of disorder; they are the bodily incarnation of *order* – the only thing capable of fighting back and holding disorder at bay. The diseases[10] of the state, Hobbes tells us in no uncertain terms, do not – and cannot – stem from the sovereign himself, given that '[t]he Soveraignty is the soul of the Common-wealth; which once departed from the Body, the members doe no more receive their motion from it' (Hobbes, 1996: 153). It is, rather, in the rabble, the multitude, the disorderly and their 'ignorance and passion' and 'Intestine Discord' (Hobbes, 1996: 153) that the causes of society's diseases lie.[11]

States, bodies, organisms and cells are all conceived as operating in a potentially hostile environment. Unwanted pathogens are then construed as something that needs to be 'fought' in both a medical *and* a political sense: individual bodies, and the body politic headed by the state, must shore up their defence mechanisms. On an individual level, this means we become individually responsible for our health. At the level of the state, emergency measures, punitive and criminalising policies, extending police powers, closing borders: all of this becomes a matter of 'self-defence', in order to win the war against the virus. Here, parallels can be drawn with the 'war on terror', where the act of naming a 'war' in itself retroactively justifies any and all measures taken by the state in the name of 'self-defence'. This usually amounts to a huge increase in military, police and executive power, the removal and abuse of human rights of large swathes of people, and massive increases in border policing and violence. This state of affairs – variously considered as states of emergency, martial law and 'the state of exception' – have, for some time now, been considered by various theorists not as 'exceptional' but as the norm.

As Walter Benjamin writes in 1940, 'the tradition of the oppressed teaches us that the "state of emergency" in which we live is not the exception but the rule. We must attain to a conception of history that is in keeping with this insight' (Benjamin, 2005). Benjamin's analysis, no less forceful today than it was in 1940, presents an exhortation to examine the state of exception through the traditions of those for whom the exception never really was an 'exception'. In other words, in order to understand how 'emergency measures' are in fact the norm (which is to say, how militarisation, policing, border control, suspension and abuse of rights, and state violence are not absent in 'peacetime', but are rather an everyday reality for those not considered to be full 'citizens'), our gaze must be trained not on the spectacle of 'emergency' powers themselves. Rather we should look to the tradition of the oppressed, that is to say the marginalised, the immigrant, the colonised, and those who find themselves 'in the face of repeated, targeted, dispossessions through the settler's armed incursion' (Harney and Moten, 2013: 17).

However systemic racism occurring at the state level is constantly disavowed through reference to formal rights and equality before the law, as well as the outlawing of racially discriminatory practices; we also see state officials publicly denouncing racism and even, in some cases, 'taking the knee', the gesture originally associated with the #BlackLivesMatter movement in the US. This means that racism and the suffering wrought by it are consistently positioned as being exceptional 'events' that must be tackled as such. Liberalism, democracy, the NHS – these things are imbued with civic value and with a political neutrality associated with 'public institutions' and organising principles. The state, neoliberalism, democracy and public health institutions are not people, and so cannot be 'racist', because 'racism', we are told, is a failure at an individual level – an attitude and something that can be identified and rooted out via 'unconscious bias training' and similar.

Yet the persistence of racial inequalities – and anti-Blackness in particular – across different temporal and geographical contexts should give us pause for thought. The pervasiveness of figures showing that Black people are not only more likely to die as a result of COVID-19, but also face disproportionate levels of policing and incarceration, demonstrates that racism goes far beyond individual attitudes. It structures the modern political landscape. The fact that racism is *structural*, however, is constantly disavowed by the state and its institutions. They insist that racism is not only an attribute of individuals, but also that those subject to racism are subject to it on an individual level, such that individuals can seek out legal redress for any discrimination they have faced. We can see this at work when, for example, Derek Chauvin (an individual US police officer) is put on trial and found guilty of the murder of George Floyd (an individual), but the machineries of state violence and police racism that allow this to happen in the first place are left intact. We are told that there is *nothing else to see here*, because the courts of law have done their duty. This is an abominable calculus, one that serves to obscure how policing functions in its everyday operations. As Sexton and Martinot write:

> Whenever one attempts to speak about the paradigm of policing, one is forced back into a discussion of particular events – high profile homicides and their related courtroom battles, for instance. The spectacular event camouflages the operation of police law as contempt, as terror, its occupation of neighbourhoods ... Both the spectacular and the subtle, against which people can unite in their desire for justice, remain the masks behind

which the daily operations of white supremacist terror proceed. (Martinot and Sexton, 2003)

What we argue, in short, is that in order to understand the Coronavirus emergency, and the policing of it, we should resist the language of 'unprecedented', we should resist the narrative of 'the event', and we should resist seeing this first and foremost as an 'exception'. While the Coronavirus itself might be novel, the state response, the policing of it, the merging of public health and public order, the huge disparities in vulnerability to the virus, and the length of time it will take some to get a vaccine compared to others – all of this has a very long history. It is a history that is being violently and continuously concealed when we hear about vitamin D deficiency and obesity as causes of sickness and death again and again, but we do not hear about the structural conditions that mean the greatest predictor of safety from this virus is whether or not you are white.

Whiteness as health, whiteness as order

Once order and health are indissolubly linked, where a disturbance to order is a 'disease' and where diseases threaten order, and where 'dangers to the integrity of the nation are increasingly biologized' (Kistner, 1999: 189), then the 'natural order' encompasses a racial hierarchy and white supremacy is left entrenched and equated with 'order'. Disturbances, rebellions, riots, resistance and protestations of this 'order' are immediately cast as disorderly, which then sets in motion the machineries of state violence to 'restore order'.

Yet it is not simply in bursts of outrage when people take to the streets that the naming and policing of disorder takes place. Indeed, in what Charles Mills terms the 'racial contract' – the origins of the modern state and its afterlives – disorder is embodied by people not considered to be white, who can be 'conceptualized in part as carrying the state of nature around with them, incarnating wildness and wilderness in their person' (Mills, 1999: 87). The state of nature is the (non-)place where self-preservation and self-defence is a natural law: states preserve this right to use violence for self-preservation. Thus, those people or places deemed *always already* embodying the state of nature, or *disorder*, are subject to pre-emptive state violence on the grounds of self-defence.

As Denise Ferreira da Silva's work shows us, modernity, far from seeing the minimisation of nature, necessity and violence sees them as intrinsically linked to the rise of juridical and scientific reason: 'raciality produces both the subject of ethical life, who the halls of law and forces of the state protect, and the subjects of necessitas, the racial subaltern subjects whose bodies and territories, the global present, have become places where the state deploys its forces of self-preservation' (da Silva, 2014: 141). Her analysis of police killings ensures that these are understood not as a result of an exclusionary operation (whereby those subject to police violence are excluded from the sphere of the universal yet to be included via enfranchisement and rights); rather, the very operations of scientific and juridical reason, ethical life, and so on, presuppose subjects of 'necessitas' for whom the full violence and self-preservation of the state is always already justified. In other words, it is not that Black people are subjected to police violence as a result of an *absence* of human rights or legal personhood but rather the very structure of rights and legal personhood are constructed via the violent operations of 'self-preservation' against those areas and people deemed 'violent'. She writes: 'the killing of Amadou Diallo in the South Bronx on 4 February 1999 was not considered an "act punishable by law" nor "injurious to the public welfare": the four officers were acquitted of two charges of second-degree murder and one charge of reckless endangerment' (da Silva, 2017: 275). No crime was said to have been committed, because of the invocation of necessity and objectivity: this killing was not, da Silva writes, a criminal act but a legal-rational one. She continues: 'For this reason, when deployed in legal decisions, the racial "laws of nature" position the black person in a moral region inhabited by subjects not governed by the rule of law, namely, in affectability' (da Silva, 2017: 277), that is without legal, political or ontological agency.

There is, then, a positioning of Black people in particular as disorderly, whether or not formal laws are transgressed. For Fred Moten, Black life constitutes an 'irreducible sociality' (Harney and Moten, 2015: 85), where Black people can be subject 'to beating and attack – whether by the state or its sanctioned, extra-governmental deputies – because … walking out alone is understood to be a threat to the order of things, a placement of that order under attack' (Moten, 2016: 140). This disorder, which always already threatens the social order, is not only assigned to Black people but to places – zones of the city where crimes are pathologised. Predominantly Black areas become assigned as 'problem areas', characterised by disorder. Kenneth B. Clark, speaking of 'ghettos', epitomises this position:

> Neither instability nor crime can be controlled by police vigilance or by reliance on the alleged deterring forces of legal punishment for the individual crimes are to be understood more as symptoms of the contagious sickness of the community itself than as the result of inherent criminal or deliberate viciousness. (Clark, 1989: 81)

Once again, crime, disease, sickness and disorder are linguistically forged together in a way that the state can use as justification for its over-policing and use of violence to restore 'order' to the body politic. Threats must be thwarted and those deemed always already a threat find themselves subject to pre-emptive violence configured as 'self-defence'. It is this logic that sees 'common good', 'public order' and 'public health' as sites where the state continues to enact anti-Black violence, both nationally and internationally. The following quote taken from Joel Olsen's text on the Jacksonian riots[12] against Black communities and abolitionists is particularly illustrative here:

> the majority were organized, disciplined, and under the leadership of the city's most prominent gentlemen. Mayors, congressmen, attorneys general, physicians, lawyers and newspaper editors directed the mobs' activities at night and defended them in the morning, often citing them as expressions of the 'will of the majority'. (Olsen, 2004: 31)

Olsen's historical analysis of slavery and democracy in the US leads him to the conclusion that 'to be a citizen was also to be white ... whiteness was not a biological status but a political color that distinguished the free from the unfree, the equal from inferior, the citizen from the slave' (Olsen, 2004: 43). Of course, the question of the US's unique relationship to democracy and slavery could be seen as rendering Olsen's analysis obsolete, when looking at the situation in the UK. Yet the point here is not that the US and the UK have identical histories in this regard, but rather that this analysis *is* relevant when we examine the uses of 'the public' in the history of law, policing and the state.

Far from a new phenomenon, we see the conflation of public health and public order, or policing as a 'public health strategy', across different times and geographical contexts. Describing a paramilitary police occupation of a favela in Brazil – supposedly a response to residents who were complaining of the difficulty of leaving their homes to be treated for dengue fever – da Silva asks: 'if the police intervened to protect residents' access to citizenship public health services, why does the choreography of the occupation only include visual and verbal signifiers of death?' (da Silva, 2014: 150). This question, as urgent now as it ever was, signals that the violence of self-preservation, natural order and public health are, of course, not new, but, we might add, have recently come under renewed intensity.

The idea that there is a 'natural' course to herd immunity, articulated both more and less explicitly by the UK and US governments, has gone hand in hand with the argument that the protection of lives through interventionist public health measures is fundamentally at odds with the needs of the economy. We find here, then, the notion of natural order rearing its head to devastating effect. As Angela Mitropoulos writes: 'Whether the right parses such deaths and illness as a result of the "invisible hand" of the market or God's divine will, either way, it is intent on describing them as inevitable and non-mournable' (Mitropoulos, 2020b). In other words the 'natural order' of households and the economy means that the unequal distribution of death appears in front of 'the law', if it appears there at all, not as a crime but as an inevitability.

The case of vaccines is also particularly illustrative here. The rush to develop a vaccine, and the successes resultant from it by Pfizer, AstraZeneca and other pharmaceutical and university bodies, was celebrated in the UK with a heavy dose of what could be termed 'vaccine nationalism'. At the time of writing, these vaccines have been hoarded by Western countries, with Canada ordering five times the amount it needs to vaccinate the whole population (Gill, 2020). The UK has since closed its borders and is rushing to vaccinate the whole population by August 2021. What is undoubtedly a worldwide problem is being responded to as a national one. Mogha Kamal Yanni, a doctor, is cited in the *British Medical Journal* as saying: 'Rich countries have enough doses to vaccinate everyone nearly three times over, whilst poor countries don't have enough to reach health workers and people at risk' (Dyer, 2020).

The unequal distribution of death is preserved and naturalised by states whose only response is heavier and heavier policing, of borders and of people. While this may be a manifestation of what Giorgio Agamben calls 'biosecurity' (Agamben, 2021: 12), we must be wary of any theorisation that does not stay attentive to the ways in which the 'health' of some is secured at the expense of others. Indeed, within this paradigm of bio-policing, the risk and vulnerability of death is not distributed evenly. That is to say, the policing of the pandemic occurs at different temporal and geographical registers: the policing of borders and the hoarding of vaccines are simply two sides of the same coin.

Public health and racism

In order to understand how structural racism permeates society, including public health, we need to acknowledge and understand its colonial roots and entanglements. Following on from our discussion of the colonial roots of policing in Chapter One, the presuppositions of public health – its methodologies, explanations and epistemologies – take us back to our discussion of medical police and the rise of populations, publics and statistics that came to the fore at the same time as scientific racism.

To be clear: we are not saying that all public health practitioners are racist. That would be to fall into the trap we have earlier identified of individualising racism. Rather, we call attention to how public health messages and practices are bound up with distinctions that perpetuate, rather than challenge, structural racism. The depoliticisation of race, its relegation to a private, *prepolitical* sphere, means that the consequences and effects of generations of racism are indexed to individual health, individual choices, and 'vulnerabilities' that tend to downplay (or exclude entirely) how anti-Blackness in particular, as well as racism more generally, impacts the health of Black people and other racialised minorities. Though speaking of the Ebola epidemic, Eugene Richardson's analysis is no less applicable to the Coronavirus itself:

Public health 'science' borrows these fabulistic tools to parse health phenomena, and in so doing imposes conservative, scientistic means for comprehending such phenomena by occulting oppressive power structures.

> This helps the privileged maintain their dominance by convincing those suffering from Ebola, for example, that they have been harmed by a virus and not by 400 years of predatory accumulation. (Richardson, 2020: 58)

This is, perhaps, the inverse of the logic we traced in Chapter One, where the 'culprit' for the spread of the virus is constructed as being people – and therefore policing and punitive measures must be taken towards them. Here, we see a slightly different, but nevertheless connected, logic at work in an approach to global health where the 'virus' is to blame for suffering and ill-health, rather than long-standing health inequalities inculcated by slavery, 'exploitative colonialism, purposeful underdevelopment, structural adjustment, resource extraction, illicit financial flows and gender violence' (Richardson, 2020: 75). In other words, the machinery of scientistic and epidemiological approaches to public health that are dominant in international and Western governmental organisations rarely, if ever, centre structural factors that mean some are much closer to death than others. As Richardson observes, when public health experts note the fact that those in the 'Majority World have worse health outcomes than those in the Global North because of hypertension, tobacco and alcohol' (Richardson, 2020: 86) but then forward no analysis of the structural causes, entire swathes of history are written out of the picture. This sort of analysis goes hand in hand with a hyper-individualised neoliberal form of governance, because those 'risk factors' can then be waved away as results of personal choices, individual lifestyles, and, at best, the failure of those respective governments to 'nudge' their citizens into having healthier lifestyles.

In May 2020, it was reported that Black people were four times more likely than their white counterparts to die from COVID-19 (Booth and Barr, 2020). The Office for National Statistics (ONS) has stated that, even controlling for what they call 'socio-economic' factors (poverty, overcrowded housing, and so on), there is still a significant, as yet unexplained 'gap' in mortality rates (ONS, 2020). The search for the 'missing' factor has led some to pontificate on 'biological' reasons for the difference (Giménez et al, 2020), such as vitamin D deficiencies. Once again, race is depoliticised, relegated to a private, individual (though somewhat intangible) 'difference' that is responsible for increasing vulnerability to COVID-19. This sort of analysis is the result of what Richardson calls the 'aura of scientificity … legitimizing synchronic, apolitical ways of cognizing outbreaks and resultant social suffering' (Richardson, 2020: 73). This way of thinking and presenting the issues has then contributed to the narrative that there is a prepolitical category of race that is at least partly responsible for the higher death rate, thus obscuring the ways in which 'webs of power/ knowledge that stretch back in time and across continents manifest as pathology in human bodies' (Richardson, 2020: 90).

Yet, journalists and popular health writers continue to individualise health conditions, to the extent that disproportionate rates of Black people dying from COVID-19 are pinned to higher rates of obesity, 'unhealthy lifestyles' and even different biology. To take but one example, Jane Brody, wrote in the *New York Times*:

> after old age, obesity is the second leading risk factor for death among those who become infected and critically ill with Covid-19. Seventy percent of American adults are now overweight, and more than a third are obese. Two other major risks for Covid, Type 2 diabetes and high blood pressure, are most often the result of excess weight, which in turn reflects unhealthy dietary and exercise habits. These conditions may be particularly prevalent in communities of color, who are likewise disproportionately affected by the pandemic. (Brody, 2021)

As Marquisele Mercedes has discussed,[13] what we see here is the 'racialising of good and bad health', moreover personalising illness as a consequence of bad lifestyle choices. Racism, Ruth Wilson Gilmore teaches, is 'the state-sanctioned or extralegal *production* and exploitation of group-differentiated vulnerability to premature death' (Gilmore, 2011: 247, emphasis added). We cannot understand the pandemic without understanding the ways in which different peoples have been *made* more vulnerable to it. We must dispense with ideas that detach individual health from structural conditions. Health is political, and whether or not you are 'healthy' is largely determined by structural factors that stretch into the past: intergenerational wealth, household income, air quality, access to services. *None* of these are individual personal choices and they will be variously impacted by class, gender and race.

The repeated references to 'underlying health conditions' is also an attempt to depoliticise the unequal risk to the virus faced by different people. Furthermore, it served initially as an attempt to calm the public and convince them of the government's *laissez faire* attitude towards the virus (Hearn, 2020). In March 2020, Boris Johnson announced that 'many more families are going to lose loved ones before their time', providing a sense of certainty and inevitability to the destruction the virus would wreak. This sense of inevitability serves to obscure the centrality of political decisions to the question of *who dies* as a result of the virus. It gives agency to the virus, configuring the virus as a force which politicians can do little about. Indeed, it is precisely the logic that Richardson posits with regard to Ebola, that tells people it is the *virus* that is killing you, not centuries of racism and sexism, decades of austerity and machineries of state violence. This narrative, espoused by politicians, was very succinctly summed up by the 'Premier of Saxony', who 'claimed recently that government policies haven't been unjust; rather the "virus is injust"' (Müller, 2021: 15).

With the emergence of the modern state, liberalism and formal rights and equality, we find race cast into the realm of the 'natural' private, prepolitical realm. The state here finds itself confronted with one of the 'natural phenomena' that affects the demography of its people, but over which it cannot exert direct control. This then privatises race (Olsen, 2004: 72) and ensures that any racial inequalities at the level of the population are seen not as an outcome of governmental *practices*, but rather as the result of private/natural or individual-level issues that the government cannot interfere with. Once racism and racial inequalities are privatised and made 'prepolitical' (Olsen, 2004: 72), the other side of this coin is that white supremacy is also *naturalised* – to the extent that its maintenance and creation via state practices is obscured. Race is connected to 'biology, ancestry, culture' (Olsen, 2004: 72) – those things that the political and public spheres exclude and that have 'no bearing on one's political and economic life' (Olsen, 2004: 72).

What, then, of the public? With household and racial inequalities deemed to be outside the political, 'the public' occupies a peculiar place. The distinction between public and private is rarely questioned, but taken as common sense. The state can – and must – *regulate* the public sphere and ensure rights and freedoms are upheld within it. The private, however, as long as you are not breaking the law, is your own. It is a sphere that is, in every sense, *non-political*; it is what grants coherence to the idea of the public, political sphere. The potency of the public, as an ideal, as an ethic, as something to be *defended*, is common in both academic and non-academic scholarship and activism. It has, in some senses, in the face of the gutting of public services by decades of neoliberal government, become a flame for the social democratic left, seeking to rally around the few state services that *are* left. Yet, as we have been arguing, the public is far from a neutral concept, but has a long and complex history that belies its modern usage. Along with police and public health, it is the 18th century which sees 'the public' as a concept, as an idea, and as a technique of government come to the fore. Foucault is again instructive in this regard:

the public, which is a crucial notion in the eighteenth century, is the population seen under the aspect of its opinions, ways of doing things, forms of behaviour, customs, fears, prejudices, and requirements; it is what one gets a hold on through education, campaigns and convictions. The population is therefore everything that extends from biological rootedness through the species up to the surface that gives one a hold provided by the public. (Foucault, 2007: 75)

In his *Lectures at the Collège de France* Foucault discusses the emergence of the 'population' as something to be managed, 'a set of processes' (Foucault, 2007: 70) that includes birth and death rates, health, hygiene, life expectancy, and so on. Crucial here, however, is that while the government must 'manage' these processes, they are subject to a range of 'natural' factors that government cannot dictate but must document and calculate. In other words, populations and all their attendant demographics *vary*, and these variations are due to a variety of reasons including climate, physical environment, 'intensity of commerce and activity in the circulation of wealth' (Foucault, 2007: 70). It is *the public*, on this reading, that offers a 'surface' on which governments can manage and regulate the 'health' of the population which subsumes everything down to the population's supposed 'biological rootedness' (Foucault, 2007: 75) up to behaviour, education, lifestyle and all that lies in between. In other words, 'the public' is what connects the government to supposedly diversifying 'natural' phenomena that occur at the level of the population. Further, the public is the mechanism that allows the government to identify, grasp and take hold of, and even transform, the behaviour and health of populations. Lest we are led to believe, however, that 'the public' naturally arises out of the population it is supposed to represent, we must be attentive to the way in which the public is *made*.[14]

We contend that the making of the public is intrinsically connected to the creation and maintenance of a white supremacist racial order. As Ulrike Kistner has argued, there is a connection between the ascendance of the population as the material and mechanism of government and scientific racism:

> the way in which, in modernity, problems of governance are being rationalized by reference to 'population': health, hygiene, fertility, birth and death rates, longevity, morbidity and mortality ... biologically based racism comes to the fore at the moment at which the biological is being drawn in the legitimation of the functioning of particular state apparatuses. (Kistner, 1999: 189)

In other words, the emergence of medical police, the 'population', life sciences and 'scientific' theories of race have entangled historical roots that see 'the biological' as something simultaneously 'natural' *and* something that must be identified, analysed, calculated and, most importantly, managed by the state. The state can then both acknowledge and dismiss disproportionate deaths from COVID-19 in the Black community as an unfortunate consequence of prepolitical inequalities – ones that, as unfortunate as they may be, the state cannot do anything about. As we have argued, however, this serves to camouflage the moments and sites where white supremacy is produced and maintained. When public health *is* police, when health and order are conflated, public health becomes one of those sites.

When we say 'public health', then, we have to demand an answer to the question: whose health? Perhaps 'the public' works to conceal the violence of the conjoining of health and order. 'Public safety' and public order have long been used as pretexts and retroactive justifications for violence against Black communities. We must also be vigilant to how calls for the state to act in the name of 'public health' can also endanger and place others at greater risk of state violence.

The catastrophic and misnamed 'herd immunity' approach that Conservative advisor and strategist Dominic Cummings has now admitted *was* government policy (despite their repeated protestations to the contrary), was pursued in the absence of a vaccine and thus constituted 'neoliberal violence' (Mitropoulos, 2020b). In a highly unequal and stratified society, allowing the virus to rip through the population means 'allowing' a disproportionate number of disabled, elderly, Black, low-paid people to die.[15] That the government, unchallenged by the media, used the phrase 'herd immunity' – a choice no doubt informed by the 'special aura' (Fine, 1993: 265) that the phrase has, along with its malleable meaning and lack of scientific consensus around it[16] – made it a key ally to those who sought to oppose stringent measures to control the virus. Once the government was forced to act, what had initially been a light-touch approach – to let the virus 'take its course' – turned into a war against the virus, with the police on the front line. Yet this is not to say that these two seemingly oppositional approaches were incompatible or contradictory. Rather, the virus itself and the policing of it, affects Black, migrant, low-paid and key workers the heaviest. Risk was essentially privatised, and those with the means, could mostly avoid it.

When calls and pronouncements to 'protect' health by 'going to war with the virus' are made, the language used should not be discounted as metaphorical or irrelevant. As Rinaldo Walcott writes:

> if you have never participated in a protest where the police are basically at war with the demonstrators then you have not fully experienced the violence that policing represents. Fully decked out in their battle gear and arranged in battalion formation, the police represent in both form and practice, a martial force arrayed against the very civilians they are supposed to protect. (Walcott, 2021a)

What this highlights is that 'protection' is conditional. The idea that the police protect 'the public' is true insofar as the public always precludes those people whom the police are policing. This then serves to legitimise the violence used by police on those people who are, by definition, not the public. This cruel logic stands behind the ostensible paradox that Walcott outlines: the police who are supposed to *protect* the public, to keep the public *safe* and to uphold *public order* can do so by going to war with those who no longer are, or never were, part of the public.

In light of this, we argue that the public is created by those who claim to serve it. By this we do not mean that the public is made up of politicians, police officers and judges, but that these people have the power to conjure the 'public' in defence of their actions and decisions (for example for reasons of *public* health or *public* order), whether or not said actions or decisions are 'popular'. What we are interested in here is the way in which the potency of 'the public' as ideal, as mythological projection, as *justification* for one's actions, is clearly not available to all. That is, 'the public' when used in political discourse, legal decisions and police activity, does not have positive content inscribed into its definition, but can be used as a device to produce different things:

1. It produces **legitimacy**. By giving the sense that concern for the public – be that safety, opinion or otherwise – state agents can de facto claim legitimacy for their actions. In reality, just by virtue of being agents of the state, they can claim to be doing something in the interests of 'the public', and thus it becomes tautological.
2. It produces **consent**. Following on from the preceding point, use of the public in this manner turns what is a 'politics by decree' into one that has supposedly been consented to. Not dissimilarly to the Hobbesian contract, once we have contracted to let state agents act in our name, they can do pretty much anything and claim that it was in the public interest.
3. It produces **whiteness**. As Joel Olsen (2004) has argued, race is not a biological category but a political one, and

one that needs to be reproduced. When the police claim to act in the name of 'public safety' and 'public order' – and those actions consistently produce racist outcomes – then the 'public' is reaffirmed as being white. White populations are affirmed as white by virtue of being the public, and this public is produced and reproduced by activities of the state which act in its name.

Despite essentially being anathema to decades of 'there is no such thing as society' style thinking and governance, as well as the government's own reluctance to lock down and an initial 'herd immunity' strategy by the back door, it seems that in general there was much more willingness to adhere to lockdown and tier restrictions than most analysts had envisaged (Reicher and Drury, 2021). Adherence has remained markedly high throughout the pandemic. Yet we must challenge the idea that this is because people are afraid of the punishment that may ensue, were they to break the rules.

Robert Reiner and others have demonstrated, through a variety of ways, that the reasons why people abstain from (certain types of) crime has very little to do with fear of punishment (Reiner, 2010). Conversely, the idea that people 'weigh up' the pros and cons of committing crime, making a rational choice to do so or not based on whether the benefits outweigh the costs (Hirshi, 1969; Becker, 1996) has also been roundly challenged by decades of scholarship (see, for example, Elster, 1979, 2000; Young, 1994, 91–7; Laibson, 1997; Jolls et al, 1998, 1538–41; Haan and Vos, 2003).

As we discuss in the following chapter, the proliferation of mutual aid networks during the pandemic points to a very different notion: that people adhere to COVID-19 rules because they *care*, not because they are afraid of the consequences were they not to do so.

THREE

Safety without police: an abolitionist provocation

Throughout this book, we have offered a rather bleak reading of how the UK government responded to the COVID-19 crisis by policing people as a virus. Thinking beyond the current moment, we also traced the social and political history of British policing – as an order maintenance institution that protects and serves the interests of the state – and challenged common distinctions between 'public health' and 'public order'. Insisting that expanded police powers under lockdown conditions are not an aberration, we argued instead that they signal an intensification of policing practices that target 'suspect populations' – and Black people in particular – for infractions of 'public order' that treat such groups as a threat to the 'health' of the state, if not 'the nation' too.

Without abandoning such a critique of the state and its coercive institutions, we end this book in a more positive and reconstructive note with what we see as a visionary world-making worldview that helps us to see a way out of this impasse. This life-giving possibility for radical change has a name: abolition(ism). But it is often given a bad name by those who offhandedly dismiss it as naive, utopian, fanciful, idealistic and unrealistic. In our effort to salvage abolitionism's reputation from naysayers, we will briefly pit it against competing views of progress and social change – while also clarifying what the term means to us, as an intellectual resource for thinking and acting differently to design public safety beyond and without policing.

Clinging to conventional wisdom or obeying the mainstream criminological hive mind makes envisaging a world without police sound foolhardy at best and sacrilegious at worst. Yet, as Kristian Williams (2015 363–4) puts it, 'it is interesting to note the things that scholars will not admit [and] the possibilities that they leave unexamined'; operating under the 'nearly universal' assumption that 'the police are a necessary feature of society' (Williams, 2015 364). Arguing against such a taken-for-granted view of policing, therefore, amounts to violating a taboo so deeply engraved on our civic conscience that it is not just indecent, but offensive too. As sociologist Rodney Stark (1972: 1) wrote in the very first page of his book on police riots: '[i]t is vulgar nonsense to be anti-police. Our society would not exist without them.'

The same sentiment was expressed with a touch of irony – yet with no less puritanical fervour – by eminent police scholar Carl Klockars (1988: 240), who similarly noted that 'no one whom it would be safe to have home to dinner argues that modern society could be police'. A few pages later, however, Klockars (1988: 257) cautions against the 'creation of immodest and romantic aspirations [about the police] that cannot, in fact, be realized in anything but ersatz terms', thereby revealing a chink in the armour of any pro-police stance – when it has no firm basis in (f)actual reality.

Naturally, we couldn't agree more. We argue that *defending* policing sounds as unthinkable to us, as abolishing it sounds to police-friendly scholars. The reason should be obvious enough. We argue for truthful accounts, community and mutual aid, justice and public safety against mythology, deceit, injustice and a sense of false security that favourable portrayals of policing provide. Instead of pretending that policing is a force for good, or being complicit in, and complacent about, the conditions of violence and harm that such pretence cultivates – we posit instead that it would be unethical to *not* make policing obsolete.

Abolish or reform?

With this provocation in mind, we break ranks with orthodox policing scholarship, in order to introduce abolitionism as a vibrant, sophisticated, holistic and radical mode of scholarship and public participation, without putting scare quotes around it or creating scarecrows out of it. Many have presented recent calls to defund and abolish police as an ideological takeover by foolishly idealistic millennial snowflakes, symbolic of a dangerous abolitionist trend that signals the end of civil(ised) debate on and off campus. Yet, abolitionism remains marginal(ised) in mainstream criminological discourse, textbooks, conferences and curricula; UK academics, in particular, 'dare not speak its name' (Ryan and Ward, 2015). Such reluctance partly reflects the reality that uttering the word results in having the ivory tower locked and bolted for fear of letting in rebellious heretics. But abolitionism is also cast out because it resides off campus as a philosophy of community organising, so it *ought* to remain outside the impregnable walls of the real estate conglomerates where (overpriced) teaching is 'delivered' like takeaway food and (undervalued) research is star-rated like hotel chains.

In challenging this defensive posture of the academic mainstream towards abolitionism, we are *not* arguing for taming or institutionalising it. We simply interrogate why naming it is considered such a terrible *faux pas*. This is an important point to insist on, because it reveals a set of assumptions about what counts as 'respectable' scholarship and what does not, even when what is 'respectable' may be disrespectful to the reality of institutions that are defended as indispensable – regardless of whether they might be founded on violence, injustice and oppression. If we were to make a sharp conceptual distinction between abolitionism and its adversaries, the battle is waged between a reformist ideology, which contends that policing may be flawed but irreplaceable, and an abolitionist framework, which argues that since policing is irredeemable given its historical and contemporary violence(s), it must be replaced by socially just alternatives.

While reformist perspectives claim that 'managing' injustice by making it more bearable should suffice, abolitionist perspectives see this logic as the very embodiment of injustice. Being the shameless abolitionists that we are, we would go as far to liken reformist agendas to a 'Lord Denningism' of sorts; a dogma expressed by Lord Denning, a former Court of Appeal judge and Master of the Rolls, who argued – in no uncertain terms – that: '[i]t is better that some innocent men remain in jail than the integrity of the English judicial system should be impugned' (Robins, 2016). Thus spoke judge Lord Denning following the wrongful conviction of six innocent men (the 'Birmingham Six') over the bombing of a Birmingham pub in one of Britain's gravest miscarriages of justice. Lord Denning nevertheless insisted that:

> If they won [the trial] it would mean that the police were guilty of perjury; that they were guilty of violence and threat; that confessions were involuntary and improperly admitted in evidence; and that the convictions were erroneous, That was such an *appalling vista* that every *sensible* person would say: 'It cannot be right that these actions should go any further'. (Woffinden, 1987: 299, emphasis added)

While reformists – following in Lord Denning's footsteps – may think it 'sensible' to justify wrongful convictions on the grounds that holding the police to account would open up 'an appalling vista', abolitionists do not content themselves with tweaking Armageddon. We wish to prevent the dramatic destruction it brings, by putting an end to it. To illustrate this divide, beyond ideological skirmishes along the reformist versus abolitionist battle line, it is worth contrasting the two perspectives in terms of the fundamental difference between them. This is no other than the crucial distinction between the means and the ends of policing. As Williams (2015 363) points out, reformist scholarship limits itself with the '*means of policing*—strategies of patrol, crowd control, interrogation techniques, use-of-force policies, organizational schemes, accountability mechanisms, morale boosters, affirmative action—while taking for granted (but rarely identifying) the *ends* of policing'. By contrast, abolitionist thinking counters that problems with policing do not arise out of a *deficit in policing procedure* but as a result of a *surplus of police* power(s).

As Vitale (2017: 7–33) painstakingly argues, the problem with policing cannot be reduced to more or better training, more workforce diversity, more procedural justice or more accountability. The problem 'with' policing is *policing* itself – its institutional and political *role*, identity, mission and function as the state's primary instrument of coercion. To (re)turn to an (over)used metaphor in policing literature, this is not a case of 'a few bad apples'. It is the tree that is poisoned and needs uprooting. Similarly, reform not only allows the underlying malaise to fester uncontrollably, but it does so by painting a veneer of action guided by 'respectability' – providing a spectacle of disinfection while leaving the infrastructure intact.

Where reformist police scholarship calls for more training, education and representation through reform, the problem becomes one of what individuals do and what reform can do to reform such individuals; essentially calling for more justice inside unjust institutions, by cautioning them to behave better while retaining all their power. A series of questions, however, remain unanswered: Who would suggest those reforms (the police, the government, or the communities that are disproportionately targeted by the police)? Who benefits from such reforms (the police, the government, or Black and other minority ethnic and other marginalised or vulnerable social groups)? What is the aim of such reforms? Do they aim to increase legitimacy and accountability of the police, by expanding their power and maintaining a favourable public image of the police? Or do they target racial and social justice?

On the opposite side of the spectrum, abolitionist thinking launches its critique at the heart of the system – not its peripheral organs – by focusing on social and racial injustice as a *default setting*, rather than a *system error*. Where reformists look to the individual for solutions to institutional problems, abolitionists aim at overthrowing the very institutions that create the problem. Where reformists devise solutions based on gathering evidence of 'best practice' and 'fairer outcomes', abolitionists ask what the institutions in question are, what they do, who do they do it to and who do they do it for; claiming that the way institutions are designed determines their function. Unless their very logic and purpose of institutions changes, superficial solutions that ignore institutional architectures can only deliver cosmetic changes that bring no real change. Where reformists work within a law enforcement approach to social problems, abolitionists prioritise social solutions to social problems through *social* rather than criminal justice. Where reformists call for better policing, abolitionists work towards disbanding, disempowering and disarming the police (McDowell and Fernandez, 2018), by replacing state regulation and social control with designing public safety anew; in ways that reflect and correspond to the needs and demands of local communities, not the interest of state agencies. Where reformism pours its energies into adding layers of procedures to unequal social structures, abolitionism aspires to make such structures redundant. Where reformists see police misconduct or miscarriage of justice as a procedural anomaly that can be ironed out with appropriate sanctions, abolitionists see policing as a fundamentally political issue that has everything to do with (state) power, rather than administrative policy. Where reformists scratch their heads to design 'just deserts' for those who offend, abolitionists ask who decides what an offence is. Where reformists see policing as neutral and apolitical, abolitionists raise questions about the role of the state in thinking about how violence can and should be responded to and accountability apportioned in ways that are not dictated by the state but by local, direct, co-operative decision making, as opposed to centralised decision-making processes. Where reformists remain convinced that reform signals progress, abolitionists maintain that reform progresses in the wrong direction by working – rather than doing away – with the institutions that are identified as needing reform. Where reformists see themselves as 'critical friends' of police (Murji, 2011), abolitionists see the police as 'our enemies in blue' (Williams, 2015. Where what Ruth Wilson Gilmore and Craig Gilmore (2008: 145) call 'reformist' reforms bolster and strengthen policing, abolitionist or 'non-reformist' reforms point to 'systemic changes that do not extend the life or breadth of deadly forces' (Gilmore and Gilmore, 2008: 145).

Such a comparison of and contrast between reformist and abolitionist approaches to policing clearly shows that the two approaches do not share a common language. Yet, paradoxically, both speak with one voice in our commitment to address and respond to violence and harm – however differently we might think about where such violence and harm comes from. Contrary to our critics, abolitionists do not advocate a free-for-all where all hell breaks loose. We, too, want to hold individuals accountable for their actions. We just don't think that calling the cops to put people in cages is an ethically justifiable or socially transformative way of doing so. We, too, want to live in safe, clean places and go about our lives without fear. We just oppose ready-made, state-driven or criminal justice definitions of what such life might, or should, look like. We, too, want justice. We just do not confuse or conflate it with vengeance – hinting at the fact that there are equally powerful emotions that create safer, restorative social environments where social relationships are based on altruism, not punishment (see, for example, Braithwaite, 1989). Rather, we argue that holding individuals accountable for their actions does not resemble policing and prisons.

Understandably, abolitionist critiques of policing and state violence may sound like airy-fairy romanticism, but so is the fantastical belief in a benevolent, caring police. However far-fetched the arguments of abolitionists may sound, is it fair to judge them against perspectives that fail to even ask the question of how we know what we know about the institutions we have? How do we know that they are just, or only occasionally violent and oppressive? Could it be that we are socialised into a logic that fails to question what we have and dare not explore what we *could* have, want or need instead? Could it be that the discomfort one feels when others suggest that familiar institutions need to be abolished comes from a fear of the unknown, preferring the devil we know to the devil we don't? Could it be that what appears so outlandish in abolitionist thinking actually betrays our opponents' lack of imagination? Could it even be that in defending the institutions that abolitionists condemn, our opponents might be pursuing their own self-interest, wilfully or unwilfully?

To answer some of those questions, it is worth spending a minute to reflect on the fact that abolitionism only calls for the abolition of unjust, violent and oppressive institutions – as it always has done in its centuries-old history. To put it differently, abolitionists today stand for the same principles and values that abolitionists stood for when they campaigned for the abolition of the slave trade and the institution of slavery too. There is nothing romantic or Pollyanna-ish about trying to end injustice. Would it be too extreme or uncompromisingly forthright to suggest that those who opposed abolitionism in the era of colonial slavery and those who oppose it today might be drawing on the same logic and the same moral justification for their thinking? While the question hangs in the air, it is worth remembering that – much as it is celebrated now, if at all – abolitionism 'back then' was rejected with the same force and arguments that are used to reject it now. Peter Fryer (1984: 64) reminds us that '[w]hen the Commons rejected Wilberforce's first motion to bring in a Bill abolishing the slave trade, in 1791, Bristol's church bells were rung, workmen and sailors were given a half-holiday, canon[s] were fired on Brandon Hill, a bonfire was lit, and there was a fireworks display'.[1] Or as a 1790 election squib had it: '[i]f our slave trade had gone, there's an end to our lives, beggars all we must be, our children and wives' (Fryer, 1984: 57–8). Worse still, as William Cowper's (1825: 13) disturbing poem *Pity for Poor Africans* goes:

> 'I own I am shock'd at the purchase of slaves [...]
> I pity them greatly, but I must be mum,
> For how could we do without sugar and rum?
> Especially sugar, so needful we see;
> What! Give up our desserts, our coffee, and tea?'

Comparisons between abolitionism's opponents then and now will undoubtedly sound offensive to many, yet the use of the term 'abolitionism' is not accidental. It emerged as a movement against colonial slavery, and it continues today as a movement against the anti-Black carceral state, the prison industrial complex and the criminal legal system. The substance of abolitionism's logic has not changed, nor have the targets of its critique; be it colonial statecraft or postcolonial state power. Abolitionists today challenge those who oppose abolition by asking simple questions about those institutions, their purpose, their function and who they harm as a result. In so doing, they draw attention to the 'deaths at the hands of state institutions such as police and their global practices such as prisons and refugee and immigration detention camps which produce Black life as a lesser life or as nonlife' (Walcott, 2021b: 12).

In this we are not suggesting that there is a precise, uncomplicated or straightforward equivalence between slavery and policing. We do, however, stress – as we did in Chapter

One – that both institutions have the same historical roots and are structured by anti-Black violence. The police, like the colonial militias out of which they emerged, still reassure and protect 'respectable', 'law-abiding' and documented citizens, property owners, the 'general public', 'deserving' victims and the state, just like they ignore the crimes of the powerful (for example, corporate or 'white-collar' crime) and they suspect minoritised groups, political activists and the 'undeserving' poor.[2] A case in point is Britain's 'hostile environment' immigration policy, defended in British courts despite its discriminatory nature on the grounds that 'such discriminatory laws' – discriminatory though they may be – are nevertheless 'in the public interest'; thereby making it clear that '"the public" is conceived of implicitly or otherwise as predominantly white' (Bain, 2021: 37).

Apart from revealing how notions of belonging are 'thrown against a sharp white background' (Hurston, 1928) to define the master category of humanity, what this example also shows is whom the state polices for and who it polices against. But it also demonstrates that those who count as deserving of protection by the state belong to the assumed and unexamined default category of the white, 'respectable', 'law-abiding', documented citizen. The rest are seen as, classified and policed as 'criminal Others' that do not belong 'here'; as well as giving rise to the term 'crimmigration' (Bhatia, 2020).

What we see here is a perfect example of criminalisation; as the logic and process by which the state classifies people according to a social hierarchy which is policed – in order to maintain the order that this hierarchy rests on. Who counts as 'decent', and who is seen as a 'threat', has less to do with what people do and more to do with the (selective) criminalisation of what people do. As much as people who dissent from this view – call them 'reformists' – might make sense of all this as immaterial (given that 'the law is the law and it ought to be respected', or at best reformed), they are at risk of forgetting how the law is made, by whom and indeed with whom in mind as needing either protection or policing. In short, the police do not just 'police'. They police *for* certain groups and *against* others, with the latter being recruited from the (lower) ranks of the marginalised and disadvantaged; be they 'raced', classed or gendered into categories of exclusion and classified as 'police property'.

Abolitionist thinking

Having raised the heat by staging an imaginary, yet no less real, confrontation between reformist and abolitionist perspectives on policing – in order to provoke some thinking about why abolitionism might not be so naive or 'dangerous' as some make out – our discussion now moves beyond mere scholarly conflict or ideological tit for tat. What follows is an attempt to present abolitionism as something bigger than a simple or single recipe that offers ready-made, off-the-shelf solutions to 'crime' and criminalisation. We want to introduce abolitionism instead as a worldview, with a rich intellectual history that embraces politics, culture, activism and community organising; thereby moving beyond and outside the sacred precincts of state administration, criminal justice policy and academia. In doing so, we intend to offer a political argument and to make an intellectual contribution, not design policy interventions – preferring to concentrate on changing intellectual gears and shifting our language and thinking on how to rethink public safety and the conditions that enable it.

The remainder of this chapter therefore offers our perspective on abolitionism, by situating it as an intellectual and political movement that emerged as a response to the transatlantic slave trade and the system of slavery, before it evolved into an attitude towards, and a framework for, analysing contemporary forms of social injustice, violence and oppression. Anchored in such history, abolitionist thinking and practice grew, by applying its insights into the present and calling for a radical reorganisation of our thinking and responses to violence away from state institutions that are themselves violent. In bringing together the intellectual history and the contemporary practice of abolitionism, we close this chapter by illustrating what abolitionism has to offer – as an invitation to create the conditions for public safety – by drawing on relevant campaigns from the US and the UK.

Unlike conventional political philosophies, abolitionism does not have a single origin story or one holy version that all abolitionists ascribe to, abide by or bow to. It does not have a symbol, a badge, a single identity or a strictly defined ideology based on a central dogma, a sacrosanct text or scripture – nor does it have an organised priesthood, divine leaders, bureaucracies or headquarters. As such, it is not even an '-ism', strictly speaking. It is a living archive of thinking, that is imbued with a radical attitude towards social change by cultivating a sensibility of making community – in ways that are not hierarchical, coercive or imposed, but negotiated and collectively arrived at. As such, it is not a far cry from anarchist thinking and organising. Yet, although both see themselves as realistic by demanding the impossible (Marshall, 1993), it would be too simplistic to argue that they are one and the same; the main difference between them being that, unlike anarchism, abolitionism emerged from the Black radical tradition (Robinson, 2020), therefore foregrounding issues of racial justice in its analysis.

This is not to suggest that anarchism is not antiracist, but to stress that not *all* streams of anarchist thought and practice *are* antiracist – as they are not all against heteronormative patriarchy. Abolitionism on the contrary, has almost always been shaped by Black radical feminist thought as an 'intellectual and political tradition' and an 'ethical intervention' (Nash, 2019: 57) that sees 'the forces of sexism and (trans)misogyny, classism and racism' as 'inextricably linked in a mutually constitutive web of oppressions and domination' (Samudzi and Anderson, 2018: 69–70; see also Lee and Rover, 2017, and Bey, 2020). Indeed, our vision for, and version of, abolitionism is wedded to the intellectual work and organising activity of Black women. These range from 19th-century figures such as Angeline Grimké, Ida B. Wells, Mary Prince, Sarah Parker Remond, Sojourner Truth and Harriet Tubman to 20th- and 21st-century protagonists such as Assata Shakur, Angela Davis, Ruth Wilson Gilmore and Mariame Kaba and many other individuals – like Pauline Hopkins, June Jordan and Toni Cade Bambara – and groups like the Organisation of Women of African and Asian Descent and the Brixton Black Women's Group. Their writing and organising may not assume the mantle of abolitionism, but their thinking betrays an abolitionist imagination. Central to such an abolitionist imagination and the radical Black feminist spirit that runs through it, is an approach to thinking and activism that sees both as connected and cross-pollinating; as vital ingredients in transformative change.

Another key element of what we might call 'the abolitionist imagination' is the focus on disentangling complex, overlapping networks of oppression and on undoing social structures that create violence and harm. Contrary to conventional thinking, abolitionists see the criminal justice system as one such harm-generating institutional network, on the grounds that it arranges intersecting institutions like policing, the courts, borders, prisons and other non-criminal legal institutions to control, punish and exclude.[3] Armed with the belief that this is a task that requires thinking and acting across scholarly, institutional, political and national borders to create change, abolitionism reflects that belief in its attitude and its approach to social change – by fusing 'vigor of thought' and 'thoughtful deed' (Du Bois, 2007: 178) and by drawing on literature, academic research, community organising and campaigning to *tear down* as well as to *build up*. Although the word 'abolitionism' itself inevitably connotes undoing, the intellectual programme of abolitionism is actually focused on *doing*; by emphasising that to abolish, the preconditions that produce what we want to abolish must be created too. As Ruth Wilson Gilmore puts it:

> Abolition is not *absence*, it is *presence*. What the world will become already exists in fragments and pieces, experiments and possibilities. So those who feel in their gut deep anxiety that abolition means knock it all down, scorch the earth and start something new, let that go. Abolition is building the future from the present, in all of the ways we can. (Gilmore and Lambert, 2019)

This view of abolitionism owes considerable intellectual debt to Black radical intellectual and activist W.E.B. Du Bois, whose magisterial work *Black Reconstruction* pointed out that although slavery may have been abolished, this was only done in the *negative* sense – by passing laws against it – not in the *positive* sense, by radically reorganising society in a way that makes processes of racial discrimination, dehumanisation, criminalisation and racial violence impossible. Seizing on this insight, modern-day abolitionists argue that abolition today needs to move away from 'emancipation' and towards 'freedom' (Walcott, 2021b); thereby calling for the uprooting of logics, and social and physical structures that create the conditions that produce social and racial injustice. In that sense, abolitionists work towards abolishing what African-American playwright Lorraine Hansberry described as 'the state of the civilization which produced that photograph of the white cop standing on that Negro woman's neck in Birmingham' (Perry, 2018). Hansberry was referring to a famous incident of racist police violence in Birmingham, Alabama, during an equally famous meeting with Attorney General Robert F. Kennedy in 1963, where Hansberry along with James Baldwin were asked to share their thoughts on civil rights. Five decades later, Harney and Moten would echo the same sentiment, by asking:

> What is, so to speak, the object of abolition? Not so much the abolition of prisons but the abolition of a society that could have prisons, that could have slavery, that could have the wage, and therefore not abolition as

the elimination of anything but abolition as the founding of a new society. (Harney and Moten, 2013: 42)

As these quotes make clear, the objective of abolition is not just to abolish the police or prisons or the criminal legal system as a whole, but to abolish the carceral, penal mindset that justifies responding to social problems with criminal legal solutions. As such, abolitionist energies are not directed solely at a list of proposed changes, but call for a change of outlook on how public safety is thought about and how public safety might be designed, through a different language and thinking that is committed to *social* justice, not criminal justice. Instead of separating thinking and action, abolitionists draw on radical thought as a resource with which to act; as a tool that can be – and is being – picked up and used by the young, Black, Queer and Indigenous people we have seen on the streets since the summer of 2020.

Moving from abolitionist theory to abolitionist practice – or rather moving closer to the crossroads where the two meet – it is worth stressing that while abolitionists share central concerns like the ones described earlier in this chapter, we don't all think alike or draw the same conclusions or roadmaps for change. Different strands of abolitionist thought make different demands, yet most agree on the need to restructure the entire institutional infrastructure of society, so that policing can be abolished – but not without addressing what makes people vulnerable and what are the social (pre)conditions that create harm. Some argue for the need to create an altogether different infrastructure of care, welfare and community support through crisis intervention teams and specialist units trained in de-escalation and conflict resolution to respond to drunken, disorderly or violent behaviour, domestic violence cases and mental health crises. Similarly, there are groups that organise around the need to recognise the social origin of most incidents of challenging, threatening and violent behaviour or trauma and respond to such incidents with social or community-oriented institutions, instead of armed and coercive ones. And, finally, there are approaches to abolitionism – like the one espoused here – which altogether reject replacing the police with another kind or form of police or policing. For example, the idea that mental health teams should either be present in policing or replace them, ignores the fact that mental health care often involves forms of carcerality and punitiveness that any project of abolitionism otherwise seeks to transform. What are sought instead are community solutions that are embedded in a 'black feminist ethic[s] of care' (Nash, 2019: 76) rather than punitive, carceral solutions focused on punishment. Such Black feminist ethics of care articulate a politics where 'states of mind, health, body and social relationships' (Noble, 2005: 135) combine to bring about freedom and justice as a result of knowing, being and doing.

The abolitionist position that we advance and work from here, therefore, is committed to an intellectual attitude, radical politics and community action that 'read[s]' and moves 'across disciplines, across continents and across communities of engagement' (Hancock, 2016: 201) to bring about social change. It is therefore approached here as a worldview and a world-making vision (which it is), rather than as a narrow doctrinaire or single-issue ideology (which it is not). As such, the version of abolitionism that we embrace is as unapologetically utopian, as it is practical and realistic. It imagines and crafts expansive 'somewheres' out of 'nowheres' – to paraphrase jazz vocalist and poet Jayne Cortez (1996) – but also works hard to disrupt, upset and show the limitations of existing ways of being in the social world that persist only 'in the absence of a precondition for [their] abandonment' (Robinson, 2016: 5).

Working towards creating such preconditions for the abandonment of the world *as it is*; involves recognising that the way the world is currently configured is patterned by inequality and social injustice that cannot be wished or legislated away. What is required instead – and abolitionism offers it — is a programme of radical change that is 'deliberately everything-ist; it's about the entirety of human environmental relations', as Ruth Wilson Gilmore put it to Rachel Kushner (Kushner, 2019). The remainder of this chapter therefore grapples with that complexity — not by offering a blueprint for global change, but by suggesting ways out of policing, criminalisation, incarceration, militarisation and institutions of state violence; as a way of thinking *out* of and *away* from them.

Doing abolitionist work, however, also requires a reckoning with the strong feelings and emotions that the police and policing evoke. Dipping into the emotional terrain that intellectual and political debates around the police bring to the surface, we discuss in turn how what the police say they *feel* during an encounter, can act as a shield against legal accountability. This leads on to discussions of feelings of sympathy or support for the police, feelings of antipathy towards the police, and thoughts on building emotional literacy for police abolition. Written as a provocation to 'circle [our] brain, fire [our] blood [and] tingle [our abolitionist] imagination', before moving 'into the arena of strife or agitation' (Moses, 1989: 246), the following section concludes the whole book by urging an encounter with what we feel about the police — and why.

Police feelings

Discussions about police are invariably emotive. The heightened calls to defund and abolish that we saw in the US and UK, summer 2020 were met with violent and vocal pushbacks from different corners of state and society. From moderates claiming that yes, there might be a problem but abolishing 'goes too far', to the far right 'Blue Lives Matter' crowd, protestors and activists have been harassed, belittled and attacked by many people who don a wide array of political stripes.

While the realm of politics has always been configured as a scene of antagonism — entangled with principles, ethics and worldviews that can be seen as needing to be 'fought for' or defended, both inside and outside formal political institutions – the law, we are told, is a different creature. Enlightenment, scientistic and legal thought tends to exclude emotions, seeing them as external to the requirements of rigour, rationality and rule of law calculus, which insists on an *impersonal* mode of governing. Liberal philosophies of state and law have elevated the idea of the 'rule of law': that when it comes to the law, everyone stands equal before it and the corollary that 'justice is blind'. These ideas stand at the forefront of modern liberal democratic states, and claim it as *the* sign of modern, progressive, fair and democratic government. As one of the exemplars and forefathers of liberalism, John Locke puts it:

> And therefore, whatever form the commonwealth is under, the ruling power ought to govern by declared and received laws, and not by extemporary dictates and undetermined resolutions; for then mankind will be in a far worse condition than in the state of nature, if they shall have armed one or a few men with the joint power of a multitude, to force them to obey at pleasure the exorbitant and unlimited degrees of their sudden thoughts, or unrestrained, and till that moment unknown wills, without having any measures set down which may guide and justify their actions: for all the power the government has being only for the good of the society, as it ought not to be arbitrary and at pleasure, so it ought to be exercised by established and promulgated laws; that both the people may know their duty, and be safe and secure within the limits of the law; and the rulers too kept within their bounds, and not be tempted, by the power they have in their hands, to employ it to such purposes, and by such measures, as they would not have known, and own not willingly. (Locke, 2003: 161)

For Locke, in order to escape the state of nature where you may be subject to the whims of 'sudden' or 'unrestrained' thoughts, we must all contract to government and the 'rule of law'. This, we are told, acts as a restraint on government as well as a condition of safety and security, where only those who break the law can be punished by agents of the law, and only within strict bounds set by lawmakers that are then written into law.

We encounter this way of thinking today where the only people who have the power to curtail or take away our 'freedom', as such, are officials of the state. These could be medical officials – with the power to section; or the police and courts – who are supposedly detecting infractions of the law and detaining those who break it; or those policing borders – the state-sanctioned organisations who have the power to detain and deport people deemed to be residing somewhere without proper authorisation. The idea that our freedom could be subject to the whims and emotions of an individual is frightening, and one that has supposedly been left behind in a distant past without government, or in far-off undemocratic or 'failed' states, where 'extrajudicial' violence by para-state organisations runs amok and where one can be arbitrarily arrested and imprisoned on the flimsiest of charges. Our freedom, by contrast, is supposedly guaranteed, unless we break the law. If this were to happen a process ensues; a judge or jury who exclude their personal feelings, by looking solely at the *facts of the case*, and only if there is evidence *beyond reasonable doubt* that you committed a crime, only then can your freedom be taken away.

The reality, however, is much different. Importantly, when it comes to killings by police, it is the *feelings* of the police – their feeling of threat and danger, posed by the person they fatally attacked – that are heard in the courtroom and that take centre-stage as retroactive justification for the violence meted out by the officer(s). For example, when looking at the testimony of Darren Wilson, the police officer in the

US who shot and killed Michael Brown, an unarmed Black man in 2014, this theatre of emotions acting as a protective shield over the officer's actions is on full display: "And when I grabbed him, the only way I can describe it is I felt like a 5-year-old holding onto Hulk Hogan". Wilson goes on to state that Brown "had the most intense aggressive face. The only way I can describe it, it looks like a demon, that's how angry he looked" (NPR, 2014). It has been well documented that Wilson was, in fact, bigger than Brown in all respects. The jury declined to charge Darren Wilson.

In 2011, Met Police Officer V53 shot and killed Mark Duggan in Tottenham, London. The officer told investigators that 'he saw a gun in Duggan's hand and felt his life to be in danger' (Forensic Architecture, 2021). It was later found that Duggan was not holding a gun while shot. An inquest jury found that the killing of Mark Duggan was a 'lawful' one because, despite Duggan not holding a gun at the time he was shot, Officer V53 *felt* that he had one, and believed he, his colleagues and 'the public' were in danger. The barrister representing the Duggan family said that the coroner had "directed the jury that the lawfulness of the lethal force, and the question of whether V53 was acting in self-defence, should be judged solely by reference to V53's honest belief as to the threat posed" (Kirk, 2017). Following the shooting, a slew of muddled and conflicting reports ensued, with the (then) Independent Police Complaints Commission (IPCC) initially announcing that Mark Duggan had shot at officers: something that turned out to be *entirely untrue*. A gun mysteriously appears 20 feet away across a fence (none of the officers saw Duggan throw the gun here and none know how it got there)[4] and an eyewitness account stated that they believed Duggan was 'executed', while holding a phone when he was killed (Casciani, 2014). It was, therefore, a matter of the officer's 'honestly held belief' that was enough to return a verdict of lawful killing. Neither example given here, of Darren Wilson nor Officer V53, is exceptional.

Phones that turn into guns. Guns that disappear and reappear in different places. Hands held up that turn into hands reaching forward. Suffocation that turns into resisting arrest. Police power as the power of transubstantiation. We now see that merely the feeling that a police officer has of threat and danger is then used as a retroactive justification for the violence then inflicted, regardless of what was actually going on. White paranoia is embodied in the figure of the police, who are ready to strike violently at anyone who is deemed threatening by virtue of their relationship to the white imaginary. Legal recognition is de facto denied to those who are presumed to be always already criminal. In response to the filmed attack on another unarmed Black man in the US, Rodney King in 1991, Judith Butler writes:

> The police are structurally placed to protect whiteness against violence, where violence is the imminent action of the black male body. And because within this schema, the police protect whiteness, their own violence cannot be read as violence; because the black male body is the site and source of danger, a threat, the police effort to subdue this body, even if in advance, is justified regardless of the circumstances. Or rather, the conviction of that justification rearranges and orders the circumstances to fit that conclusion … He is hit in exchange for the blows he never delivered, but which he is, by virtue of his blackness, always about to deliver. (Butler, 1993: 18–19)

Just as the police occupy a significant place with regard to 'the public', as discussed in the previous chapter, this is intimately connected to the particular place they occupy in relation to the law. The fact that they can shield their actions via an invocation of their 'beliefs' or 'feelings', together with their power to project 'the public' as the source of their legitimacy, becomes a potent mixture that breeds impunity. With special powers to arrest, detain and use violence against individuals, the significance and extent of police power is enormous. As discussed earlier in the context of the pandemic, borders, order and 'health' are subject to police power in ways that are not entirely new, but rather are being intensified and expanded in a renewed manner.

It is worth dwelling on the numerous ways in which police power works to continually renew its expansion – whether in the context of 'crisis' or not. As Christina Sharpe has discussed, the NYPD stop-and-frisk programme, known as 'Operation Clean Halls', gives police permission to 'roam the halls of private buildings' and describes how this has effectively placed 'hundreds of thousands of New Yorkers, mostly black and Latino, under siege in their own homes' (Sharpe, 2016: 87). The violent language of cleanliness is once again used under a pretext of 'crime-fighting'.

Seldom is it that policies are made to restrict or withdraw powers already granted to the police. Even in the face of overwhelming evidence, a police power does not 'work' in the sense of detecting or preventing crime – such as stop and search in the UK. This power saw an *increase* in use under lockdown, with Section 60 stops (that do not require 'reasonable suspicion') *doubling* compared with the same time the previous year (Marsh, 2020). The American Civil Liberties Union has gathered data and reported that the rate of police killings in the US was not slowed by the pandemic, with fatal shootings occurring 'at the same rate during the first six months of 2020 as they did over the same period from 2015 to 2019' (American Civil Liberties Union, 2020) and with the same Black, Native American/Indigenous and Latinx still at much higher rates than white people.

Feelings about police

If abolishing the police sounds frightening or worrisome to you, it is worth dwelling on the conditions that allow this feeling to take root. The idea that our health and safety *require* the police is not one that 'naturally' emerged, but was violently inculcated through centuries of political thought and statecraft that cannot be disentangled from the colonial and imperial logics that formed its crucible.

As Robert Reiner has shown, the people who feel most positively about the police are those who have the least contact with them: 'one of the most robust findings of research on public legitimation of the police is that it is much higher among those who have no direct experience of the police than those who do, whether this be as suspects, victims, witnesses, or recipients of services' (Reiner, 2010: 70). In short, if you have a positive view of the police, then it is likely that you have had very little to no contact with them. The flip-side of this is that those people who are targeted by the police, who are subject to policing and police violence on a daily basis, are not only de facto excluded from any notion of 'policing by consent', but that 'consent' to police is in itself formed on the basis of that exclusionary process. This is made clear by James Trafford who, drawing on Stuart Hall et al (1982), discusses the moral panic around mugging in the 1970s that was assigned as a 'black crime':

> the press and the courts orchestrated the link between mugging and Black youth by dramatizing deterrent sentences that were passed on specific cases. Subsequently the Metropolitan Police reconstructed their statistics backwards several years, conflated crimes that didn't belong together and *recorded data on victims' perceptions of race of their assailant.* In the mid-1970s, these statistics were released to evidence an exponential rise in mugging, principally carried out by Black young people. (Trafford, 2021: 60; emphasis added)

The double structure of this process – whereby the (white) public are invoked as being in need of protection by the police *through* anti-Black violence – is mainly ignored by said (white) public, for whom the daily toll of police violence is not felt. As Martinot and Sexton (2003: 172) note: 'for those who are not racially profiled or tortured when arrested, who are not tried and sentenced with the presumption of guilt, who are not shot reaching for their identification, all of this is imminently ignorable'. This 'ignorability' along with the *feeling* of security and safety that the police present for some, is a lethal combination. The (mostly) white public, of whom public opinion and police consent names as a source of legitimacy, is thus a public with which has very little contact with the police and very little idea about what they really do on a day-to-day basis.

Somewhat punctured though these illusions may have been recently, the outrage from white publics has proved short-lived and toothless: a horrible and predictable cycle, which sees high-profile police killings being followed by high-profile court cases and the resumption of 'business as usual'. As Vargas and James write:

> what happens when, instead of becoming enraged and shocked every time a black person is killed in the United States, we recognize black death as a predictable and constitutive aspect of this democracy? What will happen then if instead of demanding justice we recognize (or at least consider) that the very notion of justice – indeed the gamut of political and cognitive elements that constitute formal, multiracial democratic practices and institutions – produces or requires black exclusion and death as normative? (Vargas and James, 2012: 193)

Thus 'ignorability' cannot be countered simply by paying attention. It requires more than a cycle of outrage when a high-profile case comes to the fore. The acknowledgement of Black exclusion and death as normative requires an abolitionist response, because that normativity is part of the fabric of the criminal justice system.

Feeling for abolition(isms)

> In the civil stately condition all citizens are secure in
> their physical existence; there reign peace, security and
> order. This is a familiar definition of police. Modern
> state and modern police came into being simultaneously
> and the most vital institution of the security state is the
> police. (Schmitt, 1996: 31)

Abolitionist thinkers have made a distinction between safety
and security. This is paramount, when interrogating the default
reaction to the prospect of abolition – which is to invoke
security and safety, and the chaos to follow and the dangerous
people that would roam free, were we to abolish the police.
In an interview discussing this very distinction, Mariame Kaba
responds directly to those who would invoke the 'dangerous
few' as the Achilles heel of abolitionism:

> 'how are we going to deal with the rapists and the
> murderers?' This is the question that always gets thrown
> at anybody who identifies as abolitionist—and my
> question back is 'what are you doing right now about
> the rapists and the murderers?' That's the first thing: Is
> what's happening right now working for you? Are you
> feeling safer? Has the current approach ended rape and
> murder? The vast majority of rapists never see the inside
> of a courtroom, let alone get convicted and end up in
> prison. In fact, they end up becoming President. So
> the system you feel so attached to and that you seem
> invested in preserving is not delivering what you say you
> want, which is presumably safety and an end to violence.
> Worse than that it is causing inordinate additional harm.
> (Kaba and Duda, 2017)

This question of the *feeling* of safety is key. Police do not make
us safe; they offer a spectacle of *security* (to those not being

policed) presented as the presence of safety. As abolitionists so frequently accused of naive utopianism, we retort that the idea that we are made *safer* by warehousing people in appalling conditions and expecting them to be released (if they ever are) miraculously in a better position – be that rehabilitated, 'clean', less violent, less angry, more able to cope with life in this world – then it is *you*, not us, who are utopian.

In reality, prison is a violent, terrible place, where people are subject to more harm than anything else. Locking people away doesn't make us safe, it doesn't deter crime and it sure as hell doesn't help the people who go there. That these people are rendered out of sight and out of mind means that when we turn to the carceral state to 'solve' problems of violence, we are falling prey to an illusion – and a really harmful one at that.

Lawmakers and the criminal justice system as a whole create the illusion that they are carefully thinking about criminals: what should be done in response to their crimes, how it should be done and for how long. Jurisprudence and theories of punishment have been written about and pontificated on for centuries; whole libraries of thought, university departments and law firms and courts and policymakers are dedicated to thinking, writing and enacting punishment. What is the just punishment for a crime? What prison sentences do different kinds of crime *deserve*? Yet what we argue here is that doing what we do, is in fact the antithesis of any kind of thought. It is thought*less* – it couldn't be more devoid of thinking, in the sense that we, as a society, by putting people in prison, are simply turning our heads and backs, and presuming that it's fine because there *are* people who have done the thinking and acting for us, therefore we don't need to think or worry about it as a result. It is simply an 'out of sight, out of mind' approach that does absolutely nothing to solve any of the manifold problems the criminal justice system is supposedly dealing with.

At the beginning of the pandemic, reports that COVID-19 could live for days on plastic spurred a flurry of ideas about sanitising everything, from surfaces to things bought from the supermarket. Surface spread was a concern, and so businesses that were to remain open, and those that closed only to open again, reassured customers that they were doing everything they could to use antibacterial and sanitising agents on everything the customers had contact with. Shops now proudly display hand-sanitiser as you enter, and ask that you use it before entering. This has continued, despite the WHO and other health organisations stating that surface transmission, although possible, is not thought to be an issue, with one scientist saying: 'surface transmission of COVID-19 is not justified at all by the science' (Goldman in Thompson, 2020). What Derek Thompson argues in a piece for *The Atlantic* is that this is 'Hygiene Theatre'. In his words: 'this logic is warped. It completely misrepresents the nature of an *airborne* threat' (Thompson, 2020). What hygiene theatre offers, then, is the *feeling* that an establishment, or mode of transport is COVID-19 secure – it provides an enticing spectacle of cleanliness that offers people a way to feel safe when they move around the city, go out shopping or eat in a restaurant. In reality, this form of hygiene theatre is just that: theatre. It's an illusion, and one that distracts from the need for things like proper ventilation, which can be, of course, much more costly.

Staying with the theatrical for a moment, then, we can see how this logic is also at play not only with the policing of the pandemic, but also with policing in general. While originally coined to describe the vast increases in border and airport security post 9/11, the term 'security theatre' nevertheless points to a more capacious usage that is useful when we talk about the police. The idea that police keep us safe is as nonsensical as the idea that police can keep us healthy during a pandemic. As Robert Reiner has shown, 'the police are marginal to the control of crime', and further 'only a tiny fraction of crimes ever come to their attention or are recorded by them, and the overwhelming majority of these are not cleared up' (Reiner, 2010: 19), with some studies suggesting that less than a third of time on duty is spent on crime.

Police presence is thus conjured to present an illusion of safety, security and order that the state wishes to project. Or, as Rinaldo Walcott puts it, 'Policing's ultimate force and legitimacy, then, lies in its ability to make us feel secure in our everyday lives as we internalize the belief that it functions to prevent our endangerment' (Walcott, 2021a). On the other hand, it is also worth remembering that the biggest riots in recent history have occurred not as a result of an absence or withdrawal of police but the opposite – it is overpolicing, daily police violence and harassment of Black communities, and police killings that have sparked riots: Watts riots, 1965; Brixton, 1981; Los Angeles, 1992; Paris, 2005; London, 2011. *All* of these began in response to police violence. Anarchy is defined as both a condition without government and a 'state of disorder' (Oxford English Dictionary, 2006: 47). This definition defies history. Those who are really concerned about violence and 'disorder' and the 'chaos' that might ensue were we to abolish the police, would do well to look at these histories and note that police are a *source* of – and not a solution to – disorder and civil unrest.

In the wake of the killing of George Floyd in Minneapolis in May 2020 and the uprisings that occurred in response, talk of abolishing and defunding the police was thick in the air. The third precinct building of the police department was set on fire and, in June 2020, the idea of disbanding the Minneapolis Police Department was made into a serious proposition. As Charmaine Chua has written, however, a counterinsurgent wave followed, with defunding turning into 'reform' and, furthermore, with 'a sudden absence of the MPD [Minneapolis Police Department] from the streets, social workers, emergency responders, and even some community defenders have become quickly enfolded into policing work, issuing evictions, disciplining the unruly and reinforcing existing class interests' (Chua, 2020: 129).

This perhaps confirms that the problem of police goes far beyond the institution itself. There needs to be attention paid to the problem, as Frank Wilderson sees it, that 'white people are not simply "protected" by the police, they *are – in their very corporeality* – the police' (Wilderson, 2003: 20). Abolishing the police requires much more than just ridding society of the institution known as 'the police'; it requires tearing down white supremacy, and the tearing down of white supremacy requires the abolition of the police in turn.

While we have shown that the pandemic does not affect all equally, it is nevertheless highlighting the convergence between multiple crises, as well as helping to form linkages and connections locally and globally, as deathly dots are being increasingly connected. As Chua writes of the US: 'In the face of the pandemic, facing historic levels of eviction nation-wide, organizers have increasingly linked the BLM movement and the abolition of the police to the right to housing and the cancellation of rent' (Chua, 2020: 135).

The knots that tie together white supremacy, climate change, state violence, border control, poverty, ill-health and more, find themselves under a starker light, where it is increasingly being recognised that low wages, no sick pay, overwork, profit margins, homelessness and housing overcrowding, poor internet access, lack of access to public and green space – all of these undermine people's health as individuals, and also undermine the health of the collective. In the words of Fred Moten: 'the coalition emerges out of your recognition that it's fucked up for you, in the same way that we've already recognized that it's fucked up for us. I don't need your help. I just need you to recognize that this shit is killing you, too, however much more softly, you stupid motherfucker, you know?' (Harney and Moten, 2013: 140).

The abolitionist life we are already living

Political theorist James Martel argues that anarchism, far from being an embattled and precarious practice is, in fact, 'far more robust' and 'more anchored in materiality' than anything lived in, through or by the state (Martel, 2015: 188). Rather than seeing anarchism as a utopian political project, one constantly under attack and in retreat, Martel implores us to recognise where and how anarchist practices have always been around us – 'in materiality, in habit and in life patterns that are rarely deemed political' (Martel, 2015: 199). In a similar vein, we argue that the *practice* of abolitionism is not a far-flung fantastical ideal far removed from the world as we know it, but is in fact being practised in many different spaces, whether we are aware of it or not.

In recent times, and particularly since the first wave of #BlackLivesMatter uprisings in 2014, there has been an increased focus on spreading awareness about *not calling the police*. It is important to note that if your daily life is lived without impending threats of violence, this has very little, if anything, to do with the police. The corollary of this is that for many people life is, for the most part, lived without the police anyway. Economic class, race, gender, sexuality – these all render you more or less likely to encounter, or to be subject to, violence, be that material, physical, verbal, institutional or otherwise. These are also the vectors by which one is more likely to be subject to policing. These two facts are intimately connected.

Policing and prisons do nothing to address the problems of structural violence, but actually do a lot to reproduce and perpetuate them. This is why websites such as dontcallthepolice.com and rosecitycopwatch.wordpress.com are such important resources. They list housing, LBGTQ+, mental health, substances, domestic violence, among other issues and resources, navigating users to organisations they can call for help with these issues in their local area, explaining why calling the police to deal with issues such as these is more damaging than helpful, and demonstrating that alternatives to police already exist.

The concept of 'mutual aid' and its organisations long pre-exists the pandemic, but a swell of groups arising in the context of COVID-19 ensured that the term was thrust into popular discourse in a way that had not been seen before. The state is extremely wary of mutual aid. Its very existence, the fact that it is needed in so many areas, highlights that the state, far from providing people with what they need and ensuring their 'protection', safety and security, is in fact engaged in a massive operation of what Ruth Wilson Gilmore calls 'organized abandonment' (Gilmore, 2011: 257). (Remember from the previous chapter that the very *raison d'être* of the state has been construed as being the safety and wellbeing of its population.)

The case of the Black Panthers, who famously organised collectively to provide 'Survival Programs' that 'included everything from free breakfasts for school children to free sickle cell testing' (People's Kitchen Collective, 2021) is particularly illustrative. Former FBI director J. Edgar Hoover described the Black Panther Party (BPP) as: 'the greatest threat to internal security of the country'. Speaking of the free breakfasts, he said: 'The [Program] represents the best and most influential activity going for the BPP and, as such, is potentially the greatest threat to efforts by authorities to neutralize the BPP and destroy what it stands for' (in Gebreyesus, 2019).

One of the first things the BPP did when they formed was to patrol the police, in recognition of the fact that the people responsible for overseeing and holding the police accountable, are also police: 'we recognized that it was ridiculous to report the police to the police, but we hoped that by raising encounters to a higher level, by patrolling the police with arms, we would see a change in their behavior' (Newton, 2009: 127).

There was thus a visible connection between organising against police violence and the providing of goods and services through mutual aid. This connection has never disappeared. It was once again highlighted during the summer of 2020, in the midst of the pandemic and amid the protests and uprisings against the police and police violence. As Dean Spade notes:

the mutual aid projects that began mobilizing during the first months of the pandemic became vectors of participation in the growing protests. Millions of people participated in new ways in this moment – providing food, masks, hand sanitizer, medical support and protection to each other while fighting cops and white supremacists in the streets, organizing and supporting funds for criminalised people. (Spade, 2020: 209)

What this brings to light is that people are making the connections between COVID-19, racism, housing, incarceration, climate change and more in the midst of crisis. We see in these moments that multiple and converging crises need to be thought of and dealt with together, not apart. Anti-Blackness is a problem that traverses and transcends national borders, and what Saidiya Hartman (1997) calls the 'afterlives of slavery' find themselves manifesting across different temporal and geographical points – the effects of COVID-19 and the policing of it are but the latest iteration.

This is all to say that the project of abolition is expansive, and necessarily global. It is necessarily tied to working towards a world in which people have what they need, have the care that they require and don't have to fight tooth and nail simply to survive. It is radical acts and deeds that simultaneously point to the vulnerabilities and abandonment produced by the state, seek to remedy them, and by simply existing point to something *beyond* the state.

This chapter argues that moving in an abolitionist direction requires us to 'undo' policing intellectually, culturally and politically, by killing that proverbial cop inside our heads. Defunding, disarming, disbanding and disempowering the police should become a priority. Although such calls have come closer to the mainstream in the aftermath of the most recent wave of #BlackLivesMatter protests, the language of reform still dominates discussion. As Robyn Maynard argues: 'With no empirical or ethical leg to stand on, calls for *more* police reforms at this historical juncture are morally untenable: body cameras, racial diversity in hiring and implicit bias, are, after all, the conditions that nevertheless allowed for the public execution of George Floyd' (Maynard, 2020: 74).

We therefore end with five brief suggestions on how to enrich our abolitionist imagination as a practical goal – but one that cannot be achieved without a process of close reading, deep (re)thinking and reckoning with the emotional dimension of discussions about policing. The list that follows is far from exhaustive, but merely some of the things we can start doing now to move towards abolitionist practices and ways of thinking:

1. Read extensively about policing and police racism, to gain a deeper and more critical insight into both (see, for example, Hall et al, 1982; Williams, 2015; Vitale, 2017; Correia and Wall, 2018; Elliott-Cooper, 2021; Duff, 2021).

2. Don't vote for political parties that promise more powers and more money to the police – or at least do challenge them about it.

3. Learn about, join, support and organise with organisations against state and police violence such as: Netpol, Inquest, London Campaign Against Police and State Violence, Sisters Uncut, the Northern Police Monitoring Project and the United Families & Friends Campaign in the UK. Also explore global abolitionist campaign groups, such as Critical Resistance (US), Coalition Against Police Crimes and Repression (US), Abolitionist Futures (UK), #8toAbolition (US), Building the World We Want (Canada), or Taller Salud (Puerto Rico), to mention but a few.

4. Think about what we can do to be safe without the police (see, for example, Hope, 2014; Critical Resistance, 2021) and don't call the police, if possible. (The Coalition Against Police Crimes and Repression website offers a useful flowchart that lists alternatives to calling the police).[5]

5. If you are scholars, do research *on* not *for* the police. Teach policing and the history of policing differently, to illustrate

how the legacies and afterlives of colonialism and slavery still structure the criminal justice system today.

The list could go on, yet the message is simple: defunding, disarming, disbanding and disempowering the police should become a priority. Once we see that what has been presented as a remedy to the chaos and anarchy that would reign without the state and without the police is, in actuality, a characteristic of police power itself, then the notion that they uphold order, prevent crime or protect the common good can be firmly extinguished. It is then – and only then – that the work of imagining a world without police can begin.

Notes

Introduction
1   The Health Protection (Coronavirus, Restrictions) (England) Regulations 2020, Regulation 6.
2   The Health Protection (Coronavirus, Restrictions) (England) Regulations 2020, Regulation 8.
3   The Health Protection (Coronavirus, Restrictions) (England) Regulations 2020, Regulation 9.

one
1   For a searing critique of tendencies to 'naturalise' social and political problems, see Smith (2006).
2   The slogan we are referring to here, graces the front cover of this book – courtesy of photographer Saskia Vanderstichele.
3   For a similar argument, see also Brodeur (2010).
4   While the slave trade was made illegal after the British Parliament passed relevant legislation in 1807 – with effect from January 1, 1808 – slavery itself would have to wait to be (nominally) abolished with the Abolition of Slavery Bill and the Emancipation Act, which initiated the process in 1834 (see Gilmore, J. in Dabydeen et al, 2007: 2). However, although '[a]ll slaves under the age of 6 were freed immediately', the rest 'became "apprentices" for up to six years, working most of their time (for free) for their ex-owners' (Walvin, J. in Dabydeen et al, 2007: 154). In short, what started as the abolition of the slave trade in 1808 only signalled the abolition of slavery itself three decades later.
5   The term 'racial capitalism' was first used by Legassick and Hemson (1976) in the context of anti-apartheid struggles in South Africa, but became popularised by, and synonymous with, the work of Cedric Robinson (2020). To fully grasp what the 'racial' in racial capitalism refers to, capitalism has to be rethought and understood not just as a system of trade and industry, a mode of production or a phase of European economic development from

the 16th century onwards. Rather, it should be understood as a process of accumulating wealth (= capital) through the expropriation of land and the exploitation of labour, not just on European soil but in the Old Continent's colonised territories too. (Racial) capitalism, therefore, should be thought of as an economic system with a specific (geo)political history whose very nature is imperial-colonial. What makes capitalism 'racial', therefore, is the historical moment in which capitalism developed as the economic system of colonial imperialism. This imperial-colonial capitalist system of trade and industry depended on the transatlantic slave trade for buying and selling goods, which kept industries in the imperial centre going full steam ahead. To justify this profit-making trade network, a supporting ideology was necessary to rationalise the plunder of conquered lands, the extermination of indigenous people and the forced importation of slaves to plant, tend, cut and process crops. This imperial(ist) ideology was racism in its original form, before it became embedded and absorbed into contemporary social, political, economic, cultural and educational institutions – all of which have their origins in, and owe their development to, the establishment of colonial slavery at the heyday of capitalism. This is not to claim that racial classifications suddenly emerged with the expansion of imperial-colonial capitalism, but to stress that they were turbocharged during the period of European colonial conquest and unprecedented in the way such classifications determined the very humanity of the enslaved. As Robin Kelley (2017) put it, '[c]apitalism and racism ... did not break from the old [feudal] order but rather evolved from it to produce a modern world system of "racial capitalism" dependent on slavery, violence, imperialism, and genocide. Capitalism was "racial" not because of some conspiracy to divide workers or justify slavery and dispossession, but because racialism had already permeated Western feudal society.' The difference between the 'racialism' of feudal times and the 'White racism' (Drake, 2014: xi) of capitalism, therefore, is one of scale and degree. The racial 'Others' of feudal Europe wore white skins, yet were still racialised as 'inferior' and subordinate human categories (Robinson, 2020: 9–28). However, it is the advent of colonial-imperial capitalism that made racial classification its official ideology of political (mis)rule. As St Clair Drake (2014: 226) notes: '[a]lthough some negative attitudes and emotions about blackness and black people existed in Mediterranean and European cultures, these concepts did not create the system of racial slavery or the ideology that sanctioned it, White racism. That was accomplished by the capitalist system's need for a plentiful supply of low-cost labour'.

6   For critiques of 'broken windows' policing see, Roberts (1999), McArdle and Erzen (2001), Camp and Heatherton (2016), Vitale (2017) and Klinenberg (2018).

7　The Home Office website lists the 'Peelian principles' as a 'long standing philosophy of British policing': https://www.gov.uk/government/publications/policing-by-consent/definition-of-policing-by-consent

8　The term 'police property' was coined by Ed Cray (1972) and further developed by Lee (1981: 53–4), who described – in language that we do not endorse – how '[a] category becomes police property when the dominant powers of society (in the economy, polity, etc.) leave the problems of social control to the police. Let the police deal with these (n[******], queers, hippies...)'.

two

1　As we will discuss later in this chapter, and as Charles W. Mills has demonstrated, these individual rights and freedoms in liberal philosophy are, in actuality, rights and freedoms of those who are white (Mills, 1999).

2　Both Gil Andijar (2014) and O'Malley discuss the connection between blood, money and race. 'What is race', O'Malley writes, 'but a theory of purity in blood?' (O'Malley, 1994: 372).

3　This was a scheme that took place in August 2020 that offered diners a 50% discount on food purchased in restaurants and pubs.

4　See also Frey, 2020, and Mitropoulos, 2020b.

5　For a more thorough discussion, see Agamben (2015) and Lamb and Primera (2019).

6　See, for example, Tribe (1995), Neocleous (2000) and Cohen (2009).

7　Foucault is clear that 'from the seventeenth to the end of the eighteenth century, the word "police" had a completely different meaning from the one it has today' (Foucault, 2007: 312).

8　For a much more extended discussion of this point, see Lamb, M. *A Philosophical History of Police Power* (Forthcoming: Bloomsbury).

9　This is another way of paraphrasing the classic Weberian dictum that the state has the 'monopoly of the legitimate use of physical force' (Weber, 1970).

10　The association of order with health and disorder as disease has a long lineage in Western political thought, which has been traced as far back as Plato (Cavarero, 2002: 103).

11　Agamben also notes the significance of disease for Hobbes who 'in his translation of Thucydides... had come across a passage in which the plague of Athens was defined as the origin of anomia (which he translates with licentiousness) and metabole (which he renders with revolution)' (Agamben, 2015: 38). Hobbes here continues the long-standing tradition of associating political ills with ill-health and disease.

12　This was a period prior to the civil war where 'Jacksonian mobs' took part in 'riots, lynch mobs and insurrections' (Olsen, 2004: 31) across America.

Olsen notes that the majority of these 'were in defense of slavery and Black subordination' (2004: 31).

13 Some of Mercedes' writings can be found here: https://marquisele. medium.com/

14 For a relevant discussion on how 'the public' does not simply exist or arise naturally but is *made* politically, see Carrigan and Fatsis, 2021: 7–29.

15 This is confirmed by Dominic Cummings' testimony to parliament, in which a white board was shown to have written government strategies for dealing with the virus, including the phrase 'who do we not save?'.

16 As Fine notes, the threshold of vaccinated individuals needed to be reached as a percentage of population to eradicate *known* diseases such as measles is contested, and in some cases is disputed as a strategy altogether, as is the case with, for example, Variola virus (1993). In the case of SARS-CoV-2, an unknown virus without precedent, and indeed where it was not known if contracting it made one immune, or for how long, it was a breathtakingly arrogant and violent choice.

three

1 To avoid any misunderstanding, our reference to Wilberforce here does not aim to glorify him as the main or sole protagonist in the British abolitionist movement, as the story usually goes. In keeping with a similar clarification made in Chapter One – with reference to Olaudau Equiano's role in leading the way in the abolition of slavery – we should stress the roles of other Black and mixed-race abolitionists such as the 'Black Chartist' William Cuffay, William Davidson and Robert Wedderburn, to mention but a few Black anti-slavery advocates who were politically active in London.

2 This analysis owes much intellectual debt to a conference paper by Waqas Tufail – presented on 22 October 2014 at the Centre for Crime and Justice Studies. Tufail's presentation, preceded by Tim Hope's own contribution, are available at: https://www.crimeandjustice.org.uk/sites/crimeandjustice. org.uk/files/alternatives%20to%20policing%20slides.pdf

3 For a brilliant illustration of the connections between such institutions, see Davis and Dent (2001) and the website of, and relevant resources produced by, abolitionist campaigning group Critical Resistance: http:// criticalresistance.org/about/not-so-common-language/ and http:// criticalresistance.org/resources/

4 An investigation by Forensic Architecture has shown that the police and the IPCC's version of events is 'not consistent with the available spatial and biomechanical evidence' (Forensic Architecture, 2021).

5 https://44fce5f3-a0b1-4eb0-af1d-a3d9af647cae.usrfiles.com/ ugd/44fce5_f73d98f68f8846abbcef6cc2ad4e0fcf.pdf

References

Agamben, G. (2015) *Stasis: Civil War as a Political Paradigm*. Edinburgh: Edinburgh University Press

Agamben, G. (2021) *Where are We Now? The Epidemic as Politics*. London: Eris

American Civil Liberties Union (2020) 'The Other Epidemic: Fatal Police Shootings in the Time of Covid-19'. Available from: https://www.aclu.org/report/other-epidemic-fatal-police-shootings-time-covid-19?redirect=policeshootingsreport [Accessed 14 June 2021]

Andijar, G. (2014) *Blood: A Critique of Christianity*. New York: Columbia University Press

Arnold, D. (1986) *Police Power and Colonial Rule, Madras, 1859–1947*. New York: Oxford University Press

Bain, Z. (2021) 'A Very British Domination Contract?', in Gordon, F. and Newman, D. (eds) *Leading Works in Law and Social Justice*. London: Routledge, 30–47

Baker, M. and McKee, M. (2021) 'All countries should pursue a Covid-19 elimination strategy: here are 16 reasons why'. *The Guardian*. Available from: https://www.theguardian.com/world/commentisfree/2021/jan/28/all-countries-should-pursue-a-covid-19-elimination-strategy-here-are-16-reasons-why [Accessed 23 April 2021]

Baker, M.G., Wilson, N. and Blakely, T. (2020) 'Elimination could be the optimal response strategy for COVID-19 and other emerging pandemic diseases'. *BMJ*, 371: m4907

Bambara, T.C. (1992) 'Preface' in: Dash, J. (ed) *Daughters of the Dust: The Making of an African American Woman's Film*. New York: New Press

Bambra, C., Riordan, R., Ford, J. and Matthews, F. (2020) 'The COVID-19 pandemic and health inequalities', *J Epidemiol Community Health*, 74(11): 964–8

Baucom, I. (2005) *Specters of the Atlantic: Finance Capital, Slavery and the Philosophy of History*. Durham, NC: Duke University Press

Bayley, D.H. (1996) *Police for the Future*. Oxford: Oxford University Press

Becker, G.S. (1996) *Accounting for Tastes*. Cambridge, MA: Harvard University Press

Becker, H.S. (2014) *What About Mozart? What About Murder? Reasoning from Cases*. Chicago: University of Chicago Press

Bell, E. (2013) 'Normalising the exceptional: British colonial policing cultures come home', *Mémoire(s), identité(s), marginalité(s) dans le monde occidental contemporain*, *Cahiers du MIMMOC*. Available from: https://journals.openedition.org/mimmoc/1286 [Accessed 23 April 2021]

Benjamin, W. (2005) 'On the Concept of History'. Available from: https://www.marxists.org/reference/archive/benjamin/1940/history.htm [Accessed 22 May 2021]

Benton, A. (2020) 'Covid-19 interventions will become part of our social fabric'. *Africa Uncensored*. Available from: https://www.youtube.com/watch?v=BXi0CKqZ3ws&ab_channel=AfricaUncensored [Accessed 1 June 2021]

Bey, M. (2020) *Anarcho-Blackness: Notes Toward a Black Anarchism*. Edinburgh: AK Press

Bhatia, M. (2020) 'Crimmigration, imprisonment and racist violence: Narratives of people seeking asylum in Great Britain', *Journal of Sociology*, 56(1): 36–52

Booth, R. and Barr, C. (2020) 'Black people four times more likely to die from Covid-19, ONS finds'. Available from: https://www.theguardian.com/world/2020/may/07/black-people-four-times-more-likely-to-die-from-covid-19-ons-finds [Accessed 20 April 2021]

Bradley, J., Gebrekidan, S. and McCann, A. (2020) 'Waste, Negligence and Cronyism: Inside Britain's Pandemic Spending', *The New York Times*. Available from: https://www.nytimes.com/interactive/2020/12/17/world/europe/britain-covid-contracts.html [Accessed 5 January 2021]

Braithwaite, J. (1989) *Crime, Shame and Reintegration*. Melbourne: Cambridge University Press

Brodeur, J.P. (2010) *The Policing Web*. Oxford: Oxford University Press

Brody, J. (2021) 'The Pandemic as a Wake-Up Call for Personal Health'. Available from: https://www.nytimes.com/2021/03/15/well/live/pandemic-health-obesity.html [Accessed 1 June 2021]

Brogden, M. (1987) 'The emergence of the police – The colonial dimension', *British Journal of Criminology*, 27(1): 4–14

Brown, M. (2002) 'The politics of penal excess and the echo of colonial penality', *Punishment and Society*, 4(4): 403–23

Butler, J. (1993) 'Endangered/Endangering: Schematic Racism and White Paranoia', in *Uprising*, Gooding-Williams, R. (ed.) *Reading Rodney King: Reading Urban Uprising*, 15–23

Calvert, J. and Arbuthnott, G. (2021) *Failures of State: The Inside Story of Britain's Battle with Coronavirus*. London: HarperCollins

Camp, J.T. and Heatherton, C. (2016) *Policing the Planet: Why the Policing Crisis Led to Black Lives Matter*. London: Verso

Campesi, G. (2016) *A Geneaology of Public Security: The Theory and History of Modern Police Powers*. Oxon: Routledge

Carlyle, T. (1998) 'Chartism', in Guy, J.M. (ed.) *The Victorian Age: An Anthology of Sources and Documents*. London: Routledge, 155–66

Carrigan, M. and Fatsis, L. (2021) *The Public and Their Platforms: Public Sociology in an Era of Social Media*. Bristol: Bristol University Press

Casciani, D. (2014) 'Mark Duggan "did not need to die" – witness'. Available from: https://www.bbc.co.uk/news/uk-25657206 [Accessed 11 June 2021]

Cavarero, A. (2002) *Stately Bodies: Literature, Philosophy and the Question of Gender*. Michigan, MI: University of Michigan Press

Chandler, R. (1977) *The Long Goodbye*. London: Hamish Hamilton

Christie, N. (1993) *Crime Control as Industry: Towards Gulags, Western Style?* London: Routledge

Chua, C. (2020) 'Abolition is a Constant Struggle: Five Lessons from Minneapolis', *Theory and Event*, 23(4): 127–47

Clark, K.B. (1989) *Dark Ghetto: Dilemmas of Social Power* (2nd edn). Middletown, CT: Wesleyan University Press

Cohen, E. (2009) *A Body Worth Defending*. Durham, NC: Duke University Press

Cohen, P. (1979) 'Policing the Working-Class City', in *Capitalism and the Rule of Law* (ed. National Deviancy Conference). London: Hutchinson & Co., 118–36

Conn, D. (2021) 'Matt Hancock acted unlawfully by failing to publish Covid contracts', *The Guardian*. Available from: https://www.theguardian.com/society/2021/feb/19/matt-hancock-acted-unlawfully-failing-publish-covid-contracts-high-court [Accessed 23 April 2021]

Correia, D. and Wall, T. (2018) *Police: A Field Guide*. London: Verso

Cortez, J. (1996) *Somewhere in Advance of Nowhere*. New York: High Risk Books

Cowper, W. (1825) *Minor Poems, Part II*. London: John Sharpe

Craton, M. (1982) *Testing the Chains: Resistance to Slavery in the British West Indies*. London: Cornell University Press

Cray, E. (1972) *The Enemy in the Streets: Police Malpractice in America*. New York: Anchor

Cristi, R. (1998) *Carl Schmitt and Authoritarian Liberalism*. Cardiff: University of Wales Press

Critical Resistance (2021) 'Reformist Reforms vs. Abolitionist Steps to Policing', Critical Resistance. Available from: https://static1.squarespace.com/static/59ead8f9692ebee25b72f17f/t/5b65cd58758d46d34254f22c/1533398363539/CR_NoCops_reform_vs_abolition_CRside.pdf [Accessed: 8 September 2021]

da Silva, D.F. (2014) 'No-Bodies: Law, Raciality and Violence', *Meritum – Belo Horizonte*, 9(1): 119–62 da Silva, D.F. (2017) 'The Scene of Nature', in Desautels-Stein, J. and Tomlins, C. (eds) *Searching for Contemporary Legal Thought: Part II Images of the Legal Contemporary*. Cambridge: Cambridge University Press, 275–89

Dabydeen, D., Gilmore, J. and Jones, C. (2007) *The Oxford Companion to Black British History*. Oxford: Oxford University Press

Dahrendorf, R. (1985) *Law and Order*. London: Stevens and Sons

Das, D. and Verma, A. (1998) 'The armed police in the British colonial tradition', *Policing: An International Journal of Police Strategies & Management*, 21(2): 354–67

Davis, A. and Dent, G. (2001) 'Prison as a Border: A Conversation on Gender, Globalization, and Punishment', *Signs*, 26(4): 1235–41

Davis, M. (2020) 'The Monster Enters', *New Left Review*, 122: 7–14

Drake, St C. (2014) *Black Folk Here and There: An Essay in History and Anthropology, Volume 2*. New York: Diasporic Africa Press

Du Bois, W.E.B. (1936) *Black Reconstruction*. New York: Harcourt, Brace and Co.

Du Bois, W.E.B. (2007) *The Souls of Black Folk*. Oxford: Oxford University Press

Duff, K. (2021) *Abolish the Police*. London: Dog Section Press

Dyer, O. (2020) 'Covid-19: Many Poor Countries Will See Almost No Vaccine Next Year, Aid Groups Warn'. Available from: https://www.bmj.com/content/371/bmj.m4809 [Accessed 28 March 2021]

Elliott-Cooper, A. (2021) *Black Resistance to British Policing*. Manchester: Manchester University Press

Elster, J. (1979) *Ulysses and the Sirens: Studies in Rationality and Irrationality*. Cambridge: Cambridge University Press

Elster, J. (2000) *Ulysses Unbound*. Cambridge: Cambridge University Press

Emsley, C. (2013) 'Peel's Principles, Police Principles', in Brown, J. (ed.) *The Future of Policing*. Abingdon: Routledge, 11–22

Emsley, C. (2014) 'Policing the empire / policing the metropole: Some thoughts on models and types', *Crime, Histoire & Sociétés/Crime, History & Societies*, 8(2): 5–25

Ewing, K.D. (2020) 'Covid-19: Government by Decree', *King's Law Journal*, 31(1): 1–24

Fassin, D. (2013) *Enforcing Order: An Ethnography of Urban Policing.* London: Polity

Fatsis, L. (2019) 'Thinking about Knife Crime Beyond Dangerous Myths and Comfortable Untruths', *The British Society of Criminology Blog.* Available from: https://thebscblog.wordpress.com/2019/02/11/thinking-about-knife-crime-beyond-dangerous-myths-and-comfortable-untruths/ [Accessed 5 January 2021]

Fatsis, L. (2020) 'Inside the COVID-19 State: Protecting Public Health Through Law Enforcement', *The British Society of Criminology Blog.* Available from: https://thebscblog.wordpress.com/2020/04/20/inside-the-covid-19-state-protecting-public-health-through-law-enforcement/ [Accessed 8 September 2021]

Fatsis, L. (2021a) 'Policing the Union's Black: The Racial Politics of Law and Order in Contemporary Britain', in Gordon, F. and Newman, D. (eds) *Leading Works in Law and Social Justice.* London: Routledge, 137–50

Fatsis, L. (2021b) 'Sounds Dangerous: Black Music Subcultures as Victims of State Regulation and Social Control', in Peršak, N. and Di Ronco, A. (eds) *Harm and Disorder in the Urban Space: Social Control, Sense and Sensibility.* London: Routledge, Chapter 3

Fine, P. (1993) 'Herd Immunity: History, Theory, Practice', *Epidemiologic Reviews*, 15(2): 265–302

Forensic Architecture (2021) 'The Killing of Mark Duggan'. Available from: https://forensic-architecture.org/investigation/the-killing-of-mark-duggan [Accessed 12 June 2021]

Foucault, M. (1973) *The Birth of the Clinic: An Archaeology of Medical Perception.* London: Tavistock

Foucault, M. (1979) 'Omnes et Singulatim: Towards a Critique of Political Reason'. Available from: https://www.academia.edu/34116882/Michel_Foucault_Omnes_et_Singulatim_Towards_a_Criticism_of_Political_Reason_The_Tanner_Lectures_on_Human_Values_delivered_at_Stanford_University_October_10_and_16_1979 [Accessed 10 May 2021]

Foucault, M. (1995) *Discipline and Punish: The Birth of the Prison*. New York: Vintage Books

Foucault, M. (2002) 'The Political Technology of Individuals', in Faubion, J.D. (ed.) *Essential Works of Foucault 1954–1984 Volume 3: Power*. London: Penguin, 403–18

Foucault, M. (2004) *Society Must be Defended: Lectures at the Collège De France 1975–76*. London: Penguin

Foucault, M. (2007) *Security, Territory, Population: Lectures at the Collège De France 1977–1978*. Hampshire: Palgrave Macmillan

Frank, J.P. (1976) *A System of Complete Medical Police*. Baltimore: Johns Hopkins University Press

Freedland, J. (2020) 'The Magnifying Glass: How Covid revealed the truth about our world', *The Guardian*. Available from: https://www.theguardian.com/world/2020/dec/11/covid-upturned-planet-freedland [Accessed 5 January 2021]

Frey, I. (2020) '"Herd Immunity" is Epidemiological Neoliberalism'. Available from: https://thequarantimes.wordpress.com/2020/03/19/herd-immunity-is-epidemiological-neoliberalism/ [Accessed 3 May 2021]

Fryer, P. (1984) *Staying Power: The History of Black People in Britain*. London: Pluto Press

Fryer, P. (1993) *Aspects of British Black History*. London: Index Books

Gebreyesus, R. (2019) '"One of the Biggest, Baddest things We Did": Black Panthers' Free Breakfasts, 50 Years on'. Available from: https://www.theguardian.com/us-news/2019/oct/17/black-panther-party-oakland-free-breakfast-50th-anniversary [Accessed 12 June 2021]

Gill, P. (2020) 'Canada has enough COVID-19 vaccine doses to cover each citizen five times over while the fate of 67 poor countries remains undecided'. Available from: https://www.businessinsider.in/science/health/news/canada-has-enough-covid-19-vaccine-doses-to-cover-each-citizen-five-times-over-while-the-fate-of-67-poor-countries-remains-undecided/articleshow/79645493.cms [Accessed 1 April 2021]

Gilmore, R.W. (2011) 'What is to be done?', *American Quarterly*, 63(2): 245–65

Gilmore, R.W. and Gilmore, C. (2008) 'Restating the Obvious', in Sorkin, M. (ed.) *Indefensible Space: The Architecture of the National Insecurity State*. New York: Routledge, 141–62

Gilmore, R.W. and Lambert, L. (2019) 'Making Abolition Geography in California's Central Valley', *The Funambulist*. Available from: https://thefunambulist.net/magazine/21-space-activism/interview-making-abolition-geography-california-central-valley-ruth-wilson-gilmore [Accessed 2 January 2020]

Gilroy, P. and Sim, J. (1987) 'Law, Order and the State of the Left', in Scraton, P. (ed.) *Law, Order and the Authoritarian State*. Milton Keynes: Open University Press, 71–107

Giménez, V., Inserra, F., Ferder, L., García, J. and Manucha, W. (2020) 'Vitamin D Deficiency in African Americans is Associated with a High Risk of Severe Disease and Mortality by Sars-CoV-2'. Available from: https://www.nature.com/articles/s41371-020-00398-z [Accessed 20 May 2021]

Goveia, E.V. (1960) 'The West Indian Slave Laws of the Eighteenth Century', *Revista de Ciencias Sociales*, IV: 75–105

Haan, W. de and Vos, J. (2003) 'A crying shame: the over-rationalized conception of man in the rational choice perspective', *Theoretical Criminology*, 7(1): 29–54

Hall, S. (1979) 'The Great Moving Right Show', *Marxism Today*, January, 14–20

Hall, S., Critcher, C., Jefferson, T., Clarke, J. and Roberts, B. (1982) *Policing the Crisis: Mugging, the State and Law and Order*. London: Macmillan

Hamlin, C. (2006) 'William Pulteney Alison, the Scottish philosophy, and the making of a political medicine', *Journal of the History of Medicine and Allied Sciences*, 61(2): 144–86

Hancock, A.M. (2016) *Intersectionality: An Intellectual History*. New York: Oxford University Press

Harney, S. and Moten, F. (2013) *The Undercommons: Fugitive Planning and Black Study*. New York: Minor Compositions

Harney, S. and Moten, F. (2015) 'Michael Brown', *Boundary 2*, 42(4): 81–7

Hartman, S. (1997) *Scenes of Subjection: Terror, Slavery and Self-Making in Nineteenth-Century America.* Oxford: Oxford University Press

Hearn, K. (2020) 'People with "Underlying Conditions" are Being Treated as Expendable. But Our Lives Matter'. Available from: https://www.theguardian.com/commentisfree/2020/mar/19/underlying-conditions-coronavirus-health [Accessed 15 May 2021]

Hirshi, T. (1969) *Causes of Delinquency.* Berkeley: University of California Press

Hobbes, T. (1996) *Leviathan.* Cambridge: Cambridge University Press

Hope, T. (2014) 'What Are the Alternatives to Policing' *Centre for Crime and Justice,* Available from: https://www.crimeandjustice.org.uk/news/what-are-alternatives-policing [Accessed: 5 January 2021]

Hulsman, L. (1986) 'Critical criminology and the concept of crime', *Contemporary Crises,* 10(1): 63–80

Hurston, Z.N. (1928) 'How It Feels to be Colored Me'. Available from: http://xroads.virginia.edu/~MA01/Grand-Jean/Hurston/Chapters/how.html (Accessed 4 May 2021)

Jackson, N. (2016) 'Imperial suspect: Policing colonies within "post"-imperial England', *Callaloo,* 39(1): 203–15

James, C.L.R. (2013) *Modern Politics.* Oakland, CA: PM Press

Jolls, C., Sunstein, C.R. and Thaler, R. (1998) 'Behavioural approaches to law and economics', *Stanford Law Review,* 50: 1471–550

Kaba, M. (2020) 'To Stop Police Violence We Need Better Questions – and Bigger Demands'. Available from: https://gen.medium.com/to-stop-police-violence-we-need-better-questions-and-bigger-demands-23132fc38e8a [Accessed 1 May 2021]

Kaba, M. and Duda, J. (2017) 'Towards the Horizon of Abolition: A Conversation with Mariame Kaba'. Available from: https://thenextsystem.org/learn/stories/towards-horizon-abolition-conversation-mariame-kaba [Accessed 15 June 2021]

Kelley, R.D.G. (2016) 'Black Study, Black Struggle'. *Boston Review.* Available from: http://bostonreview.net/forum/robin-d-g-kelley-black-study-black-struggle [Accessed 5 January 2021]

Kelley, R.D.G. (2017) 'What Did Cedric Robinson Mean by Racial Capitalism?'. *Boston Review*. Available from: http://bostonreview.net/race/robin-d-g-kelley-what-did-cedric-robinson-mean-racial-capitalism [Accessed 23 April 2021]

Kelling, G.L. and Wilson, J.Q. (1982) 'Broken Windows: The police and neighborhood safety', *The Atlantic*. Available from: https://www.theatlantic.com/magazine/archive/1982/03/broken-windows/304465/ [Accessed: 5 January 2021]

Kirk, T. (2017) 'Mark Duggan's Family Lose Bid to Overturn Lawful Killing Verdict'. Available from: https://www.standard.co.uk/news/london/mark-duggan-s-family-lose-bid-to-overturn-lawful-killing-verdict-a3501811.html [Accessed 10 June 2021]

Kistner, U. (1999) 'Georges Cuvier: Founder of Modern Biology (Foucault) or Scientific Racist (Cultural Studies)?', *Configurations*, 7(2): 175–90

Klinenberg, E. (2018) *Palaces for the People: How to Build a More Equal and United Society*. London: The Bodley Head

Klockars, C. (1988) 'The Rhetoric of Community Policing', in Greene, J.R. and Mastrofski, S.D. (eds) *Community Policing: Rhetoric or Reality*. New York: Praeger, 239–58

Knemeyer, F.L. and Trib, K. (1980) 'Polizei', *Economy and Society*, 9(2): 172–96

Kushner, R. (2019) 'Is Prison Necessary? Ruth Wilson Gilmore Might Change Your Mind', *The New York Times*. Available from: https://www.nytimes.com/2019/04/17/magazine/prison-abolition-ruth-wilson-gilmore.html [Accessed 4 May 2021]

Laibson, D. (1997) 'Golden eggs and hyperbolic discounting', *Quarterly Journal of Economics*, 112(2): 443–77

Lamb, M. and Primera, G. (2019) 'Sovereignty between the Katechon and the Eschaton: Rethinking the Leviathan', *Telos*, 187(Summer): 107–27

Lawrence, D. (2020) *An Avoidable Crisis. The Disproportionate Impact of Covid-19 on Black, Asian and Minority Ethnic Communities: A Review by Baroness Doreen Lawrence*. Available from: www.lawrencereview.co.uk [Accessed 23 April 2021]

Lee, B. and Rover, R. (2017) *Night-Vision: Illuminating War and Class on the Neo-Colonial Terrain*. Montreal: Kersplebeded

Lee, J.A. (1981) 'Some Structural Aspects of Police Deviance in Relations with Minority Groups', in Shearing, C. (ed.) *Organizational Police Deviance*. Toronto: Butterworths, 49–82

Legassick, M. and Hemson, D. (1976) 'Foreign Investment and the Reproduction of Racial Capitalism in South Africa', *Anti-Apartheid Movement*, September, 2–16

Liberty (2020) 'Joint Letter on Policing Regulations'. Available from: https://www.libertyhumanrights.org.uk/wp-content/uploads/2020/05/2020_05_28_Joint-Letter-Policing-Regulations.pdf [Accessed 15 May 2021]

Liberty (2021) *The Protect Everyone Bill*. Available from: https://www.libertyhumanrights.org.uk/wp-content/uploads/2020/04/LIBERTY-Protect-Everyone-Bill-FINAL-reduced-size.pdf [Accessed 23 April 2021]

Linebaugh, P. (2006) *The London Hanged: Crime and Civil Society in the Eighteenth Century*. London: Verso

Loader, I. (2020) *Revisiting the Police Mission*. Policing Insight Paper 2, The Strategic Review of Policing in England and Wales. The Police Foundation. Available from: https://policingreview.org.uk/wp-content/uploads/insight_paper_2.pdf [Accessed 23 April 2021]

Locke, J. (2003) *Two Treatises of Government and a Letter Concerning Toleration*. London: Yale University Press

Macpherson, C.B. (2011) *The Political Theory of Possessive Individualism: Hobbes to Locke*. Oxford: Oxford University Press

Marsh, S. (2020) 'Met Police Increased Use of Section 60 Stop and Search During Lockdown'. Available from: https://www.theguardian.com/uk-news/2020/jul/27/met-police-increased-use-of-section-60-stop-and-search-during-lockdown [Accessed 15 June 2021]

Marshall, P. (1993) *Demanding the Impossible: A History of Anarchism*. London: Fontana

Martel, J. (2015) 'The Anarchist Life We are Already Living', in Moran, B. and Salzani, C. (eds) *Towards the Critique of Violence: Walter Benjamin and Giorgio Agamben*. London: Bloomsbury, 187–201

Martinot, S. and Sexton, J. (2003) 'The avant-garde of white supremacy', *Social Identities*, 9(2): 169–81

Maynard, R. (2020) 'Police Abolition/Black Revolt', *Topia: Canadian Journal of Cultural Studies*, 41: 70–8

McArdle, A. and Erzen, T. (2001) *Zero Tolerance: Quality of Life and the New Police Brutality in New York City*. New York: New York University Press

McDowell, M.G. and Fernandez, L.A. (2018) 'Disband, Disempower, and Disarm': Amplifying the Theory and Practice of Police Abolition', *Critical Criminology*, 26(3): 373–91

McQuade, B. and Neocleous, M. (2020) 'Beware: Medical Police', *Radical Philosophy,* 2.08(Autumn): 3–9. Available from: https://www.radicalphilosophy.com/wp-content/uploads/2020/09/rp208_mcquade_neocleous.pdf [Accessed 22 January 2021]

Mills, C.W. (1999) *The Racial Contract*. London: Cornell University Press

Mitropoulos, A. (2020a) *Pandemonium: Proliferating Borders of Capital and the Pandemic Swerve*. London: Pluto Press

Mitropoulos, A. (2020b) '"Herd Immunity" was Originally about Vaccination. Now it is Neoliberal Violence'. Available from: https://truthout.org/articles/herd-immunity-was-originally-about-vaccination-now-it-is-neoliberal-violence/ [Accessed 22 April 2021]

Monbiot, G. (2021) 'What's as scary as Covid? The fact our leaders still have no plan to control it', *The Guardian*. Available from: https://www.theguardian.com/commentisfree/2021/jan/13/scary-covid-leaders-no-plan-to-control-pandemic-cycle [Accessed 22 January 2021]

Moses, W.J. (1989) *Alexander Crummell: A Study of Civilization and Discontent*. New York: Oxford University Press

Moten, F. (2016) 'Jurisgenerative Grammar (for alto)', in Lewis, G.E. and Piekut, B. (eds) *The Oxford Handbook of Critical Improvisation Studies, Volume 1*. Oxford: Oxford University Press, 128–42

Müller, J.-W. (2021) 'Blame Brussels', *London Review of Books*, 43(8)

Murji, K. (2011) 'Working Together: Governing and Advising the Police', *The Police Journal*, 84(3): 256–71

Musu, C. (2020) 'War Metaphors used for Covid-19 are Compelling but also Dangerous'. Available from: https://theconversation.com/war-metaphors-used-for-covid-19-are-compelling-but-also-dangerous-135406 [Accessed 20 May 2021]

Nash, J. (2019) *Black Feminism Reimagined: After Intersectionality*. Durham, NC: Duke University Press

Neocleous, M. (2000) *The Fabrication of Social Order: A Critical Theory of Police Power*. London: Pluto Press

Netpol (2020) *'Britain is Not Innocent'*. Available from: https://secureservercdn.net/50.62.198.70/561.6fe.myftpupload.com/wp-content/uploads/2020/11/Britain-is-not-innocent-web-version.pdf [Accessed 23 April 2021]

Newton, H.P. (2009) *Revolutionary Suicide*. New York: Penguin Books

Noble, D. (2005) 'Remembering Bodies, Healing Histories: The Emotional Politics of Everyday Freedom', in Alexander, C. and Knowles, C. (eds) *Making Race Matter, Bodies, Space and Identity*. Basingstoke: Palgrave Macmillan

NPCC (National Police Chiefs' Council) (2021) 'Fixed Penalty Notices Issued under Covid-19 Emergency Health Regulations by Police Forces in England and Wales'. Available from: https://policingthecoronastate.files.wordpress.com/2021/03/fpn-update-npcc-feb-2021.pdf [Accessed 3 May 2021]

NPR (2014) 'Ferguson Documents: Officer Darren Wilson's Testimony'. Available from: https://www.npr.org/sections/thetwo-way/2014/11/25/366519644/ferguson-docs-officer-darren-wilsons-testimony [Accessed 10 June 2021]

Ogborn, M. (1993) 'Ordering the City: Surveillance, Public Space and the Reform of Urban Policing in England 1835–56', *Political Geography*, 12(6): 505–21

Olsen, J. (2004) *The Abolition of White Democracy*. Minnesota, MN: University of Minnesota Press

O'Malley, M. (1994) 'Specie and Species: Race and the Money Question in Nineteenth-Century America', *The American Historical Review*, 99(2): 369–95

ONS (Office for National Statistics) (2020) 'Why have Black and South Asian People been Hit Hardest by Covid-19?'. Available from: https://www.ons.gov.uk/peoplepopulationandcommunity/healthandsocialcare/conditionsanddiseases/articles/whyhaveblackandsouthasianpeoplebeenhithardestbycovid19/2020-12-14 [Accessed 3 June 2021]

Oxford English Dictionary (1989) 2nd ed. Oxford: Clarendon Press.

Oxford English Dictionary (2006) Oxford: Oxford University Press

Pearson, A. (2020) 'We need you, Boris – Your health is the health of the nation'. Available from: https://www.telegraph.co.uk/women/politics/need-boris-health-health-nation/ [accessed 1 June 2021]

People's Kitchen Collective (2021) 'History of the Black Panther Party'. Available from: http://peopleskitchencollective.com/panthers-history [Accessed 12 June 2021]

Perry, I. (2018) 'Lorraine Hansberry, American radical: She pushed RFK to make "a moral commitment" on civil rights', *Salon*. Available from: https://www.salon.com/2018/12/09/lorraine-hansberry-american-radical/ [Accessed 4 May 2021]

Plato (1994) *The Republic*. Oxford: Oxford University Press

Platt, T. (2015) 'Obama's Task Force on Policing: Will It Be Different This Time?', *Social Justice: A Journal of Crime, Conflict & World Order*. Available from: http://www.socialjusticejournal.org/obamas-task-force-on-policing-will-it-be-different-this-time/ [Accessed 23 April 2021]

Rayner, G. (2020) 'Boris Johnson to Press Ahead with Back to Work Campaign Despite Rise in Coronavirus Cases'. Available from: https://www.telegraph.co.uk/politics/2020/09/12/boris-johnson-press-ahead-back-work-campaign-despite-rise-coronavirus/ [Accessed 25 May 2021]

Reicher, S. and Drury, J. (2021) 'Pandemic Fatigue? How Adherence to Covid-19 Regulations has been Misrepresented and why it Matters'. Available from: https://blogs.bmj.com/bmj/2021/01/07/pandemic-fatigue-how-adherence-to-covid-19-regulations-has-been-misrepresented-and-why-it-matters/ [Accessed 1 May 2021]

Reiner, R. (2010) *The Politics of the Police*. Oxford: Oxford University Press

Reiner, R. (2016) *Crime*. London: Polity

Richardson, E.T. (2020) *Epidemic Illusions: On the Coloniality of Global Public Health*. Massachusetts, MA: MIT Press

Robert, A. (2020) 'Lessons from New Zealand's COVID-19 outbreak response', *The Lancet Public Health*, 5(11): e569–e570

Roberts, D.E. (1999) 'Race, Vagueness, and the Social Meaning of Order-Maintenance Policing', *Faculty Scholarship at Penn Law*, 589

Robins, J. (2016) 'It's not the system that's wrong. It's the bastards on the bench', *The Justice Gap*. Available from: https://www.thejusticegap.com/paddy-hill-its-not-the-system-thats-wrong-its-the-bastards-on-the-bench/ [Accessed 3 May 2021]

Robinson, C.J. (1984) 'An Inventory of Contemporary Black Politics', *Emergency*, 2: 21–8

Robinson, C.J. (2016) *The Terms of Order: Political Science and the Myth of Leadership*. Chapel Hill: The University of North Carolina Press

Robinson, C.J. (2020) *Black Marxism: The Making of the Black Radical Tradition*. Chapel Hill: The University of North Carolina Press

Ryan, M. and Ward, T. (2015) 'Prison Abolition in the UK: They Dare Not Speak Its Name?', *Social Justice*, (41)3: 107–19

Samudzi, Z. and Anderson W.C. (2018) *As Black as Resistance: Finding the Conditions for Liberation*. Edinburgh: AK Press

Schmitt, C. (1996) *The Leviathan in the State Theory of Thomas Hobbes: Meaning and Failure of a Political Symbol*. London: Greenwood Press

Seigel, M. (2018) *Violence Work, State Power and the Limits of Police*. Durham, NC: Duke University Press

Sharpe, C. (2016) *In the Wake: On Blackness and Being*. London: Duke University Press

Smith, N. (2006) 'There's No Such Thing as a Natural Disaster'. *Understanding Katrina: Insights from the Social Sciences*. 11 June. Available from: https://items.ssrc.org/understanding-katrina/theres-no-such-thing-as-a-natural-disaster/ [Accessed 8 September 2021]

Spade, D. (2020) *Mutual Aid: Building Solidarity During This Crisis (And the Next)*. London: Verso Books

Stark, R. (1972) *Police Riots: Collective Violence and Law Enforcement*. Belmont, California: Wadsworth Publishing Company

Stewart, H. and Sample, I. (2020) 'Coronavirus: enforcing UK lockdown one week earlier "could have saved 20,000 lives"', *The Guardian*. Available from: https://www.theguardian.com/world/2020/jun/10/uk-coronavirus-lockdown-20000-lives-boris-johnson-neil-ferguson [Accessed 5 January 2021]

Storch, R. (1975) 'The Plague of Blue Locusts: Police Reform and Popular Resistance, 1840-57', *International Review of Social History*, 20(1): 61–90

Storch, R. (1977) 'The Problem of Working-Class Leisure: Some Roots of Middle-Class Moral Reform in the Industrial North: 1825-50', in Donajgrodzki, A.P. (ed.) *Social Control in Nineteenth Century Britain*. London: Croom Helm, 138–62

Storch, R. (1993) 'The Policeman as Domestic Missionary: Urban Discipline and Popular Culture in Northern England, 1850-80', in Morris, R. and Rodger. R. (eds) *The Victorian City: A Reader in British Urban History, 1820–1914*. London: Longman, 281–306

Syal, R. (2021) 'English Covid rules have changed 64 times since March, says barrister', *The Guardian*. Available from: https://www.theguardian.com/world/2021/jan/12/england-covid-lockdown-rules-have-changed-64-times-says-barrister [Accessed 12 January 2021]

Tarizzo, D. (2017) *Life: A Modern Invention*. Minneapolis: University of Minnesota Press

Taylor, D. (1997) *The New Police in Nineteenth-Century England: Crime, Conflict and Control*. Manchester: Manchester University Press

Taylor, D. (2021) 'Priti Patel's detention policies found to breach human rights rules', *The Guardian*. Available from: https://www.theguardian.com/uk-news/2021/apr/14/priti-patels-detention-policies-found-to-breach-human-rights-rules [Accessed 23 April 2021]

Terpstra, M. (2020) 'From the King's Two Bodies to the People's Two Bodies: Spinoza on the Body Politic', *Early Science and Medicine*, 25(1): 46–71

REFERENCES

Thompson, D. (2020) 'Hygiene Theater is a Huge Waste of Time'. Available from: https://www.theatlantic.com/ideas/archive/2020/07/scourge-hygiene-theater/614599/ [Accessed 16 June 2021]

Thompson, E.P. (1966) *The Making of the English Working Class*. New York: Vintage Books

Tilly, C. (1992) *Coercion, Capital, and European States AD 900–1992*. Cambridge: Blackwell

Toscano, A. (2020) 'The State of the Pandemic', *Historical Materialism*, 28(4): 3–23

Toynbee, P. (2021) 'Why has Britain become numb to the horror of deaths caused by incompetence?', *The Guardian*. Available from: https://www.theguardian.com/commentisfree/2021/jan/07/britain-deaths-incompetence-coronavirus-boris-johnson [Accessed 22 January 2021]

Trafford, J. (2021) *The Empire At Home: Internal Colonies and the End of Britain*. London: Pluto Press

Tribe, K. (1995) *Strategies of Economic Order: German Economic Discourse 1750–1950*. Cambridge: Cambridge University Press

Vargas, J.C. and James, J. (2012) 'Refusing Blackness-as-Victimization: Trayvon Martin and the Black Cyborgs' in Yancy, G. and Jones, J. (eds) *Pursuing Trayvon Martin: Historical Contexts and Contemporary Manifestations of Racial Dynamics*. New York: Lexington Books, 193–205

Vitale, A.S. (2017) *The End of Policing*. London: Verso

Walcott, R. (2021a) *On Property*. Ontario: Biblioasis

Walcott, R. (2021b) *The Long Emancipation: Moving Toward Black Freedom*. London: Duke University Press

Wall, T. (2020) 'The police invention of humanity: Notes on the "thin blue line"', *Crime Media Culture*, 16(3): 319–36

Walvin, J. (2011) *The Zong: A Massacre, the Law and the End of Slavery*. New Haven, CT: Yale University Press

Weber, M. (1970) 'Politics as a Vocation' Available from: https://open.oregonstate.education/sociologicaltheory/chapter/politics-as-a-vocation/ [Accessed 1 May 2020]

WHO (World Health Organization) (2020) 'WHO Director-General's statement on IHR Emergency Committee on Novel Coronavirus (2019-nCoV)'. Available from: https://www.who.int/director-general/speeches/detail/who-director-general-s-statement-on-ihr-emergency-committee-on-novel-coronavirus-(2019-ncov) [Accessed 5 January 2021]

Wilderson, F. (2003) 'The Prison Slave as Hegemony's (Silent) Scandal', *Social Justice*, 30:(2): 18–27

Williams, E. (1996) *Capitalism and Slavery*. New York: Capricorn Books

Williams, K. (2015) *Our Enemies in Blue: Police and Power in America*. Edinburgh: AK Press

Williams, P.J. (1993) *The Alchemy of Race and Rights*. London: Virago

Williams, R. (2003) 'A state of permanent exception: The birth of modern policing in colonial capitalism', *Interventions*, 5(3): 322–44

Woffinden, B. (1987) *Miscarriages of Justice*. London: Hodder and Stoughton

Yates, T. (2020) 'Why is the government relying on nudge theory to fight coronavirus?', *The Guardian*. Available from: https://www.theguardian.com/commentisfree/2020/mar/13/why-is-the-government-relying-on-nudge-theory-to-tackle-coronavirus [Accessed 5 January 2021]

Young, J. (1994) 'Incessant Chatter: Recent Paradigms in Criminology', in Maguire, M., Morgan, R. and Reiner, R. (eds) *The Oxford Handbook of Criminology*. Oxford: Oxford University Press, 69–124

Index

References to endnotes show both
the page number and the note number (231n3).